The Weight Watchers Cookbook 2024

A collection of 80 wholesome recipes to help you lose weight without sacrificing taste + budget-friendly tips for navigating meal planning. Includes veggies options and diabetes-friendly dishes.

Edyth Breese

The Weight Watchers Cookbook 2024

Copyright © [Edyth Breese] 2024

All rights reserved. No part of this book may be reproduced or transmitted in any form or by any means, electronic or mechanical, including photocopying, recording, or by any information storage and retrieval system, without written permission from the copyright holder.

Disclaimer

The information provided in "Weight Watchers Cookbook 2024" is for general informational purposes only. While every effort has been made to ensure accuracy and completeness, the author/publisher assumes no responsibility for errors, inaccuracies, or omissions. Individuals using the recipes or advice contained in this cookbook are responsible for their own health and well-being. Consult with a healthcare professional or nutritionist for personalized guidance. The author/publisher disclaims any liability for damages or injuries resulting from the use of the information presented in this cookbook.

Edyth Breese

The Weight Watchers Cookbook 2024

MEET EDYTH BREESE

Edyth Breese is a devoted chef and nutrition expert who ardently advocates for healthful living by crafting savory, nutrient-rich meals. Her culinary path is distinguished by innovation and a deep grasp of dietary principles, allowing her to merge her enthusiasm for gastronomy with a commitment to health promotion.

In her role as a chef, Edyth demonstrates a broad expertise in various global cuisines, consistently emphasizing the preparation of dishes that satisfy the palate while enhancing health. Her inventive culinary style showcases her insight into the intricate interplay of taste and health benefits.

As a nutritionist, Edyth has cultivated a greater respect for the impact of conscious food choices. Her approach is grounded in the belief that feeding the body involves more than simply monitoring caloric intake; it's about making knowledgeable, enjoyable decisions that pave the way for a lasting, healthful way of life.

The Weight Watchers Cookbook 2024

What you'll find in this book

01 Introduction - 11

- Welcome Message - 11
- Understanding Weight Watchers and Smart points - 12
- Budget friendly tips for navigating recipes and meal planning - 13
- Importance of a balanced and mindful approach to eating - 15

02 Scrumptious Breakfast - 17

- Banana Pancakes - 21
- Poached egg and avocado on toast - 22
- Colcannon cakes with fried eggs - 23
- Berry baked Oats with Coconut - 25
- Baked Oat Waffles - 26
- Ham and Potato hash with poached eggs - 27
- Cheesy waffles with homemade baked beans - 28
- Nutty breakfast bites - 30
- Fromage Frais with granola and berries - 31
- Beetroot and egg hash - 32
- Egg and Bacon Roll - 34
- Cheese and tomato breakfast muffins - 36
- Porridge with blueberries - 37
- Smoked Salmon Rosti - 38
- French toast crumpet with blueberry compote - 40

03 Lunchtime delights - 41

- Curried butternut Squash soup - 45
- Baked vegetable Frittata - 46
- Mushroom soup - 48
- Roasted veg and tuna salad - 50
- Aubergine pizza slices - 51
- Asian Style Turkey Salad - 53
- Mushroom and ham frittata with potato salad - 55
- Warm Kale and Chicken Salad - 57
- Beef and Paprika soup with Soured cream - 59
- Beetroot and Mackerel toastie - 61
- Mushroom 'pizzas' with wedges - 62
- Roasted Pepper Crumpet Pizza - 64
- Cauliflower, Coconut and Tumeric Soup - 66
- Greek style orto salad - 67

04 Dinner Feasts - 69

- Chicken Lentil and Kale Braise - 73
- Mustard Glaze Salmons with Lentils - 74
- Prosciutto-wrapped haddock with celeriac mash - 76
- Boodles with Harissa meatballs - 78
- Tofu pho - 80
- Mushroom & Spinach Spaghetti - 82
- India Style vegetable Stir-fry - 84
- Griddled rump steak with Chios & Mustard Mayo - 86
- Gluten-free beef Lasagne - 88
- French Onion Risotto - 90
- Lentil Bolognese & sweet potato - 92
- Prawn Singapore noodles - 94

The Weight Watchers Cookbook 2024

05 Delectable Desserts - 97

- Strawberry ripple mouse cake - 101
- Mini Strawberry cheesecakes - 103
- Chai Shortbread - 104
- Spiced Satsuma roulade - 106
- Banana and walnut loaf - 108
- Red velvet cupcakes - 109
- Apricot, blueberry and nit crumble - 111
- Cheats trifle - 112
- Plum Amaretto pudding - 113
- Toffee apple pie - 115
- Steamed lemon pudding - 116
- Apple and Rhubarb crumble - 118
- Cranachan - 120

06 Vegetarian Options - 121

- Shakshuka - 125
- Sweet corn and Carrot Fritters - 127
- Veggie Frittata Slice - 129
- Caprese Panini rolls - 131
- Veggie delight salad - 133
- Veg and chilli tofu rolls - 135
- Veggie hash with poached eggs - 136
- Vegetarian lasagne - 138
- Sweet and sour cauliflower with rice - 140

07 Diabetes Friendly Recipes - 143

- Banana berry parfait - 147
- Creamy oat porridge with apple and blueberries - 148

- Buckwheat pancakes with honeyed ricotta - 149
- Honey and ginger chicken stir-fry - 151
- Coconut pancakes - 153
- Dark chocolate avocado cake - 154
- Greek-inspired chicken burgers - 156
- Strawberry and cottage cheese muffins - 158
- Easy chicken curry - 160

08 Smoothie recipes - 163

- Chocolate-pineapple protein smoothie - 167
- Chocolate-strawberry protein smoothie - 168
- Vanilla-strawberry protein smoothie - 169
- Chocolate-banana protein smoothie - 170
- Apple & greens smoothies - 171
- Cherry-almond smoothies - 172
- Chocolate Almond & Cherry Smoothie - 173
- Creamy corn smoothie - 174

09 Conclusion - 175

10 Your Feedback Matters! - 177

Introduction

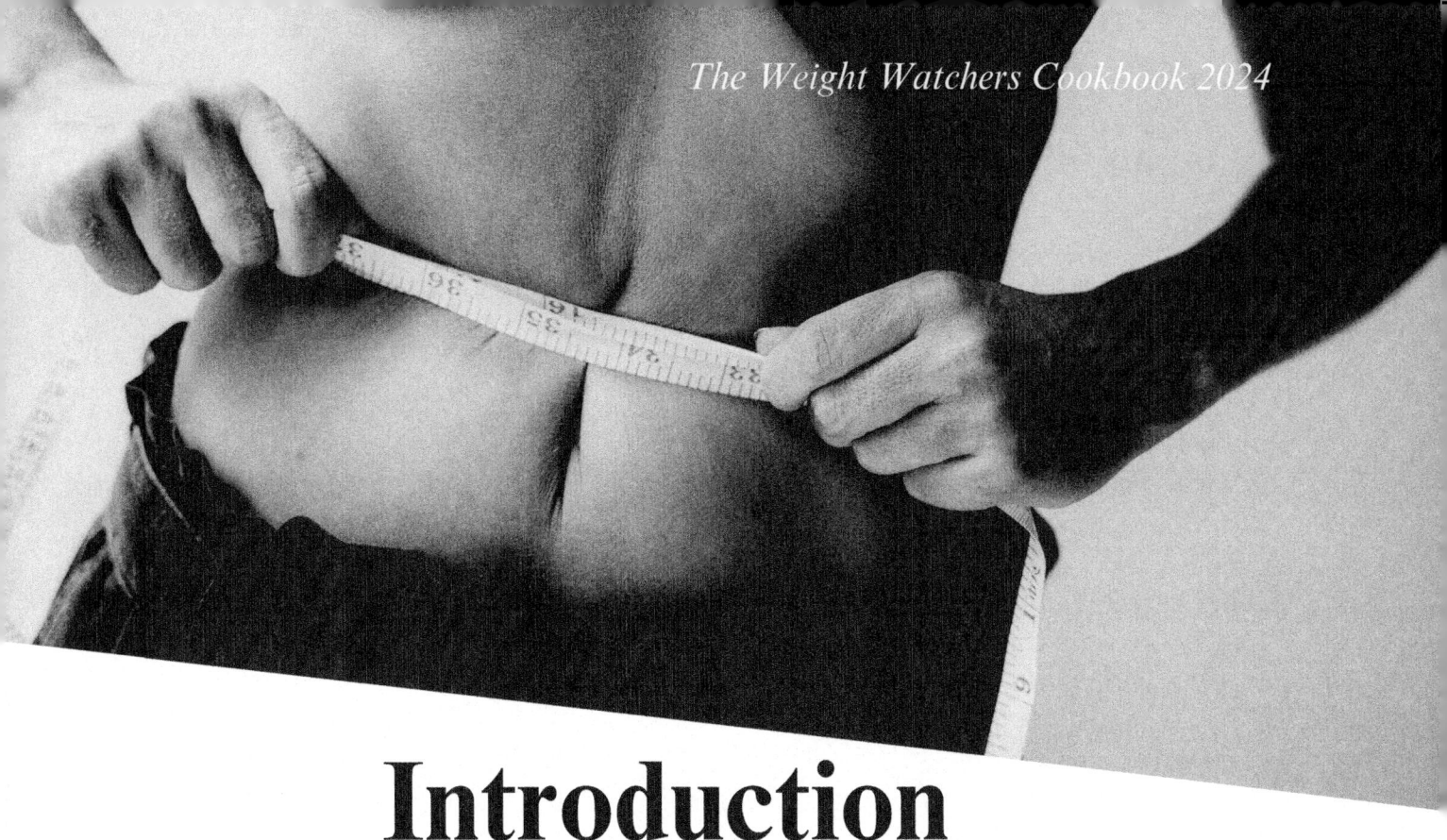

Welcome to the Weight Watchers Cookbook 2024, your gateway to a tantalizing and health conscious culinary adventure. Amidst a plethora of dietary fads, weight watchers shines as a symbol of health-conscious culinary adventure. Amidst a plethora of dietary fads, Weight Watchers shines as a symbol of achievable and enduring health practices. This book is more than a mere assortment of dishes; it is your ally in conscious eating and a testament to the joy of nutritious cuisine.

At the heart of Weight Watchers is the belief that every bite matters, with a point system designed to steer your eating habits. As you turn the pages of this cookbook, you'll encounter an array of carefully selected recipes for every occasion. Whether you're craving a hearty breakfast, a sumptuous dessert, or looking for dishes that cater to diabetic or gluten-free lifestyles, there's a spectrum of flavors to suit your dietary needs and desires.

Each creation is not just a treat for your taste buds but also a reflection of the enduring principles behind Weight Watchers' triumph. As you embrace the balance of wholesome eating, allow this cookbook to be your guide to a life of vitality. Prepare to indulge in the richness of taste, adopt a vibrant way of living, and transform every dining experience into a festivity of health and flavor.

Understanding Weight Watchers and SmartPoints

WW, formerly known as Weight Watchers, is built upon a series of guiding principles designed to encourage lasting weight management and nurture a positive connection with food. These principles are the foundation for making smart food choices while still enjoying a diverse diet. Let's explore the core concepts of WW:

Points-Based Nutrition

Each food is given a points value based on its nutritional makeup. The goal is to keep within a daily points budget.

Eating with Freedom

All foods can be eaten; the plan promotes balance. It emphasizes controlling portions and choosing wisely within your points range.

Foods with Zero Points

Some foods have zero points to highlight their nutritional value. It promotes eating more fruits, veggies, lean proteins, and beans.

Incorporating Exercise

Physical activity is part of the program, tracked with FitPoints. Rewards are given for a variety of exercises, supporting a comprehensive health strategy.

Community Support

WW offers a network of support through group sessions, online chats, and tech-based tools. It also fosters a sense of accountability and camaraderie with peers on similar paths.

Conscious Eating

The progra. encourages being attentive to eating patterns and mindful at meal times. It focuses on enjoying the taste of food and being attuned to hunger and satisfaction signals.

Strategies for Behavioral Change

It focuses on behavioral tactics to maintain progress while aiding in building better habits and managing the emotional aspect of eating.

Wellness Beyond the Scale

It Promotes overall well-being, not just weight loss and highlights other benefits like more vitality, better moods, and improved general health.

Budget friendly tips for navigating recipes and meal planning

Cooking on a budget and meal prepping doesn't have to feel like a high-wire act in the kitchen. With some smart strategies, you can sail through recipes and create tasty, cost-effective dishes that satisfy both your taste buds and your budget. Ready your shopping list, and let's jump into action!

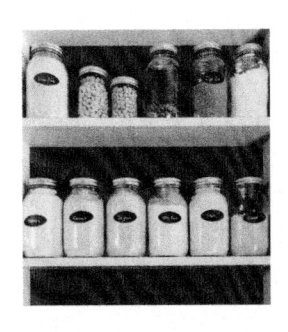

1. Stock Your Pantry Wisely:

Consider your pantry a treasure chest of economical champions. Keep it filled with multi-purpose items such as beans, lentils, pasta, rice, canned tomatoes, and frozen veggies. These staples can be the backbone of numerous dishes, making your budget go further while sparking your culinary imagination.

2. Commit to a Weekly Menu:

Crafting a meal plan for the upcoming week is a smart move for your wallet. It curbs spontaneous purchases, maximizes the use of leftovers, and encourages buying in larger quantities (often at reduced prices). Plus, it curtails the temptation for last-minute takeout.

3. Reinvent Your Leftovers:

Don't view leftovers as reheated repeats; see them as a blank slate for innovation! Get creative and repurpose them. Turn that leftover roasted chicken into a zesty salad or a comforting pot pie. Give yesterday's pasta a new life in a frittata or a warming soup. Your budget will thank you for your inventiveness!

4. Opt for Seasonal Shopping:

Seasonal produce isn't just tastier; it's also more wallet-friendly. When fruits and veggies are in their prime, they're generally more abundant and less expensive. So, take advantage of what the season offers and let the fresh, local produce inspire your meals.

5. Become a Pro at Swapping Ingredients:

If a recipe includes a costly item, don't stress. Become adept at making swaps. Try lentils instead of ground beef in your chili, tofu in place of expensive shrimp in your stir-fry, or go for frozen berries over fresh in your smoothies. The tasty outcomes might surprise you!

6. Cook in Large Batches:

Preparing meals in large quantities is a thrifty lifesaver. Whip up a sizable batch of soup or chili and divide it for lunches or speedy dinners during the week. Roast a big chicken and use the leftovers in various ways. Large-scale cooking is a time-saver and a budget stretcher.

7. Go Meat-Free More Often:

Cutting back on meat consumption can make a noticeable difference in your food expenses. Dive into the world of vegetarian and vegan dishes that don't skimp on flavor or protein. Ingredients like lentils, beans, tofu, and tempeh are economical powerhouses that can be turned into a plethora of hearty meals.

8. Spice Things Up Yourself:

Skip the costly sauces and pre-made spice mixes. Instead, curate your own collection of spices and become a kitchen chemist. Play with different herbs and spices to concoct your own unique dressings and marinades. It's a cost-saving technique that adds an individual flair to your cooking.

Importance of a Balanced and Mindful Approach to Eating

Embracing a thoughtful and well-rounded approach to nutrition is key to nurturing overall health, building a positive connection with our meals, and aiding in steady weight control. This strategy is so important for the following reasons:

Diverse Nutrients

Eating a variety of foods guarantees a wide spectrum of essential nutrients, which are vital for our body's proper functioning. A mix of different food types offers the necessary vitamins, minerals, and additional nutrients for our well-being.

Caloric Harmony

Matching the calories we consume with those we burn is crucial for a healthy body mass. Conscious eating enables us to tune into our body's signals for hunger and satiety, helping to avoid both overeating and underconsumption.

Sustainable Weight Goals

Quick-fix diets and severe restrictions might yield immediate results but often fail in the long run. A balanced method encourages lasting weight control through feasible and ongoing lifestyle adaptations.

Mind and Body Synergy

Eating with awareness strengthens the bond between our mental and physical states. Focusing on the sensory experiences of food, like its flavor and texture, enriches the enjoyment of meals.

Emotional Health

Mindful eating increases our sensitivity to the emotional reasons behind our food choices. Recognizing these triggers allows for healthier emotional responses and decreases the tendency to use food as a source of comfort.

Digestive Health

A varied diet rich in different foods promotes effective digestion. Adding fiber-filled options helps keep the digestive tract in good shape.

Lowered Deficiency Risks

A balanced diet reduces the chances of missing out on important nutrients, which boosts overall health. Fulfilling our nutritional requirements strengthens the immune system, bone density, and other bodily functions.

Consistent Energy

Well-proportioned meals help in delivering a steady flow of energy all day. By avoiding sharp blood sugar spikes and drops, we can keep our energy stable.

Healthy Lifestyle Practices

Adopting a thoughtful and balanced eating pattern fosters the growth of enduring, healthy habits. It supports a lasting and constructive engagement with our dietary choices.

The Weight Watchers Cookbook 2024

Scrumptious Breakfast

to get you started

Edyth Breese

- Banana Pancakes
- Poached egg and avocado on toast
- Colcannon cakes with fried eggs
- Berry baked Oats with Coconut
- Baked Oat Waffles
- Ham and Potato hash with poached eggs
- Cheesy waffles with homemade baked beans
- Nutty breakfast bites
- Fromage Frais with granola and berries
- Beetroot and egg hash
- Egg and Bacon Roll
- Cheese and tomato breakfast muffins
- Porridge with blueberries
- Smoked Salmon Rosti
- French toast crumpet with blueberry compote

Edyth Breese

The Weight Watchers Cookbook 2024

Banana Pancakes

2 Points

Preparation Time : 15 min	Total time : 20 min
Cook Time : 5 min	Servings : 2

Ingredients

- Banana - Two of medium size; mash one and a half, slice the other half.

- Whole Egg - Three of medium size; beat them well.

- Pure Vanilla Extract - Just a half teaspoon, keep it level.

- Baking Powder - A scant quarter teaspoon.

- Cinnamon Powder - A small dash will do.

- Nutmeg Powder - Roughly one gram, or a quick pinch.

- Low-Calorie Cooking Spray - Four quick spritzes.

- Agave Nectar - One tablespoon, nice and even.

- Fresh Blueberries - About 80 grams.

Preparation Steps

- Grab a bowl of medium size and whisk together your mashed banana, beaten eggs, vanilla essence, baking powder, and a pinch each of cinnamon and nutmeg until it's all nicely blended.

- Heat a sizable non-stick skillet over medium flame after giving it a light coating with the low-cal cooking spray.

- For each pancake, ladle about two tablespoons of the batter into the pan. You might have to cook in several rounds.

- Allow them to sizzle for a minute or two until you see the edges firm up and the underside turn a lovely shade of brown, then nimbly flip them over with a slender spatula and let them brown on the other side for an additional minute. Carry on with the rest of the batter in the same way.

- Once your delightful banana pancakes are ready, crown them with a few slices of banana, a handful of blueberries, and a generous swirl of agave syrup. Serve up this regal breakfast and enjoy a meal that's truly fit for royalty!

Poached egg & Avocado on toast

5 Points

- Preparation Time : 5 min
- Total time : 10 min
- Cook Time : 5 min
- Servings : 1

Ingredients

- Low-Calorie Brown Bread - 1 slice
- Ripe Avocado - 70g, lightly mashed
- Whole Raw Egg - 1 medium size
- Red Pepper Flakes - a dash

Preparation Steps

- Begin by toasting a slice of low-calorie brown bread until it reaches your desired level of crispness. Once toasted, uniformly spread the lightly mashed ripe avocado atop the bread.

- For the egg, bring a pot of water to a gentle simmer and carefully break the egg into the water. Allow it to poach for approximately 3 minutes or until the egg whites have solidified while ensuring the yolk remains tender and runny.

- To complete the dish, carefully place the softly poached egg on the avocado toast. Garnish with a dash of red pepper flakes and add salt and pepper according to your preference. Enjoy your nutritious and flavorful meal.

The Weight Watchers Cookbook 2024

Colcannon cakes with fried eggs

4 Points

Preparation Time : 20 min   **Total time : 1 hr**

Cook Time : 40 min   **Servings : 4**

Ingredients

- Potatoes, uncooked - 500 grams, Maris Piper variety, chopped into small pieces

- Brussels sprouts, uncooked - 150 grams, finely sliced

- Cabbage - 100 grams, Savoy variety, finely sliced

- Ground Nutmeg - 1/4 teaspoon, leveled

- All-purpose Flour - 20 grams

- Low-calorie oil spray - 4 pumps

- Shallots - 2 medium-sized, minced

- Spinach - 450 grams, tender leaves

- Eggs, whole, uncooked - 4 medium-sized

Preparation Steps

- Start by boiling a sizeable pot of water over a medium flame. Cook the potato chunks for 15-20 minutes until they soften. Include the shredded Brussels sprouts and cabbage during the final 3 minutes of boiling. Once done, drain and let the vegetables sit in the pot to dry off with the steam for a short while.

- Mix in the ground nutmeg and proceed to mash the mixture until the potatoes turn creamy and the other vegetables are somewhat integrated. Season according to your preference. Let the mixture cool down a bit before forming it into 8 equal-sized cakes.

- Preheat your oven to 120°C (fan-assisted 100°C, gas mark ½). Spread the flour on a broad plate and gently coat each cake with it. Use the low-calorie spray to lightly grease a large skillet and cook the cakes over a medium flame for about 4-5 minutes on each side until they achieve a golden hue. Afterward, transfer them to a baking tray and place them in the oven to stay warm.

- Clean the skillet and apply another round of the oil spray. Cook the minced shallots for about 3 minutes until they turn soft, adding a little water if necessary to prevent drying out. Introduce the spinach and stir for roughly 2 minutes until it wilts, which might require adding the spinach in two parts. Season as desired. Move the spinach to a bowl, cover to retain warmth.

- For the final step, clean the skillet once more, spray with the oil, and fry the eggs for 2-3 minutes until the egg whites are fully set but the yolks remain runny.

- To Serve, plate each potato and vegetable cake with a portion of the warm spinach on the side, topped with a fried egg. Finish with a dash of freshly ground black pepper for added flavor.

The Weight Watchers Cookbook 2024

Berry-baked oats with coconut

5 Points

Preparation Time : 5 min　　**Total time : 40 min**

Cook Time : 35 min　　**Servings : 6**

Ingredients

- Rolled Oats – 150 grams

- Whole Eggs – 3 medium-sized, beaten lightly

- Nonfat Plain Yogurt – 350 grams, additional for topping

- Ground Cinnamon – 2 level teaspoons

- Agave Nectar – 2 level tablespoons

- Pure Vanilla Extract – ½ level teaspoon

- Assorted Frozen Berries – 250 grams, additional for topping

- Shredded Coconut – 2 tablespoons

Preparation Steps

- Begin by preheating your oven to 200°C (392°F) for a conventional oven, 180°C (356°F) for a fan-assisted oven, or Gas Mark 6.

- In a mixing bowl, combine the rolled oats, beaten eggs, nonfat plain yogurt, ground cinnamon, agave nectar, and pure vanilla extract.

- Carefully fold in the majority of the mixed berries, reserving some for garnish.

- Transfer the mixture into a baking dish measuring approximately 22cm x 14cm

- Sprinkle the remaining berries and shredded coconut on top of the mixture.

- Place the baking dish in the oven and bake for 30 to 35 minutes, or until the top of the oats starts to turn golden brown.

- Serve the baked dish warm, garnished with additional nonfat plain yogurt and berries.

Baked Oat Waffles

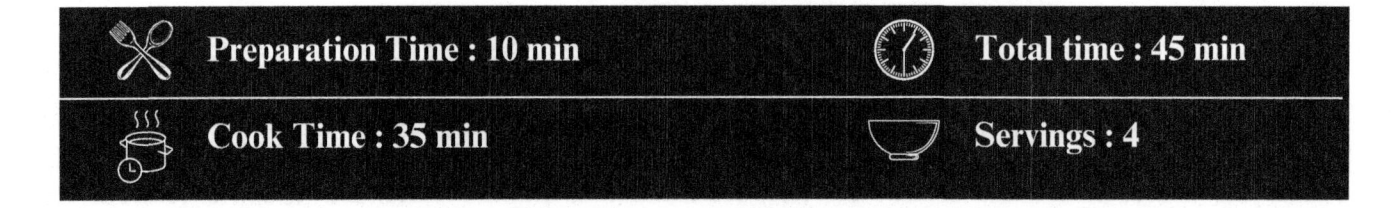

4 Points

- Preparation Time: 10 min
- Total time: 45 min
- Cook Time: 35 min
- Servings: 4

Ingredients

- Rolled Oats - 100 grams
- Leavening Agent (Baking Powder) - 1 level teaspoon
- Fine Sea Salt - ¼ teaspoon
- Cinnamon Powder - ½ level teaspoon
- Partially Skimmed Milk - 125 milliliters
- Ripe Bananas - 2 medium, pureed
- Low-Calorie Oil Spray - 4 pumps
- Plain Greek Yogurt (Nonfat) - 100 grams
- Fresh Blueberries - 100 grams
- Pure Honey - 2 level teaspoons

Preparation Steps

- Begin by heating your oven to a temperature of 180°C (or 160°C with a fan, gas mark 4). In a mixing vessel, stir together the rolled oats, baking powder, salt, and ground cinnamon. Create a depression in the center of the dry ingredients, then pour in the milk and add the mashed banana, whisking until you achieve a smooth, uniform batter.

- Position a silicone waffle mold (with space for 4 waffles) on a cookie sheet and evenly distribute the batter into the mold. Transfer to the oven and bake for 30 to 35 minutes, or until the waffles are fully baked and the edges have become golden and crisp.

- Allow the waffles to rest in the mold for a short interval before transferring them to serving dishes. Garnish each waffle with a generous spoonful of the nonfat Greek yogurt and scatter the fresh blueberries on top. Finish by lightly drizzling honey over the waffles just before serving.

Ham & potato hash with poached eggs

4 Points

Preparation Time: 5 min
Total time: 25 min
Cook Time: 20 min
Servings: 4

Ingredients

- Low-calorie non-stick cooking spray (4 spritzes)
- One small red onion, thinly sliced
- 500 grams of boiled potatoes, chopped into small chunks
- 150 grams of high-quality ham, diced
- A few drops of spicy pepper sauce (such as Tabasco), adjusted to your preference
- Four medium-sized whole, raw eggs
- A handful of fresh parsley, coarsely chopped

Preparation Steps

- Coat a sizeable nonstick skillet with the low-calorie cooking spray and sauté the red onion with a bit of ground black pepper until it becomes tender, which should take about 6 to 8 minutes.

- Introduce the boiled potato chunks and diced ham into the skillet, warming them thoroughly. Mix in a little of the spicy pepper sauce and continue cooking for about 5 minutes until the potatoes develop a light golden crust.

- In the meantime, gently poach the eggs in simmering water for approximately 2 to 3 minutes.

- Evenly distribute the potato and ham mixture into serving dishes and carefully place a poached egg on top of each. Embellish with a scattering of chopped fresh parsley and a final seasoning of ground black pepper before serving.

Cheesy waffles with homemade baked beans

5 Points

Preparation Time: 15 min
Total time: 50 min
Cook Time: 35 min
Servings: 4

Ingredients

- Low-calorie cooking spray - 2 sprays
- Rolled oats - 125 grams
- Baking powder - 1 level teaspoon
- Reduced-fat milk - 125 milliliters
- Whole eggs - 3 large
- Reduced-fat Cheddar cheese, grated - 1 medium portion
- Salt - 1/4 teaspoon
- Onion, finely chopped - 1 medium
- Light brown sugar - 1 teaspoon
- Chopped canned tomatoes - 2 large cans
- Half a vegetable stock cube - to make 200 ml of vegetable stock
- Worcestershire sauce - 1 tablespoon
- Paprika - a pinch

Preparation Steps

- Preheat your oven to 180°C (fan-assisted 160°C, gas mark 4). Lightly coat a 4-hole silicone waffle mold with cooking spray and place it on a baking sheet.

- In a food processor, combine half of the oats with the baking powder, milk, eggs, cheese, and salt. Process until you have a smooth batter, then pour it into a mixing bowl and fold in the remaining oats. Fill the waffle mold with the batter and bake for 30-35 minutes, or until the waffles are firm and the edges are beginning to turn golden.

- For the bean topping, lightly spray a non-stick frying pan with cooking spray. Sauté the diced onion over medium heat for 6-8 minutes until softened. Mix in the brown sugar, chopped tomatoes, prepared vegetable stock, Worcestershire sauce, and paprika. Season to your liking. Allow the mixture to simmer for 5 minutes, then add the beans and continue to simmer for another 5 minutes until the sauce thickens.

- Cooked cannellini beans - 2 large cans, drained
- Serve the baked waffles with a generous topping of the bean mixture and a light dusting of paprika.

Nutty breakfast bites

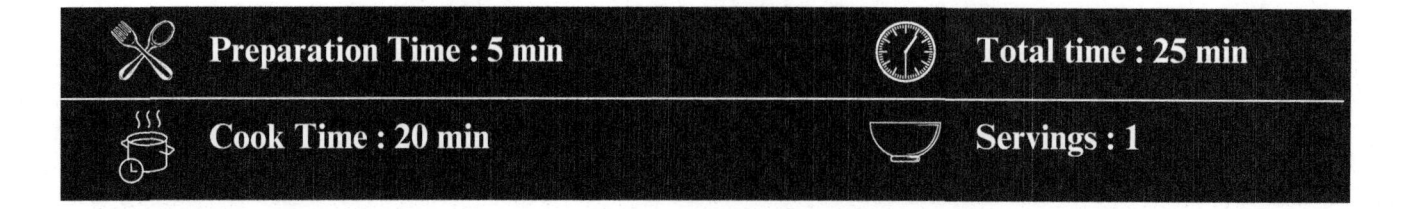

5 Points

Preparation Time: 5 min
Cook Time: 20 min
Total time: 25 min
Servings: 1

Ingredients

- One whole, raw egg
- A serving of porridge oats
- Half of a medium banana, mashed
- 7 grams of sultanas
- 4 grams of powdered peanut butter
- Half of a medium banana, sliced (for garnish)
- 7 grams of cashew nuts (for garnish)

Preparation Steps

- Begin by preheating your oven within the range of 180°C to 200°C (356°F to 392°F). Prepare a baking sheet by lining it with parchment paper.

- In a mixing bowl, combine the whole raw egg, porridge oats, mashed banana, sultanas, and powdered peanut butter until the mixture is uniform.

- Transfer the mixture onto the lined baking sheet using a spoon. Garnish with banana slices and cashew nuts.

- Place the baking sheet in the oven and bake for approximately 15 to 20 minutes, or until the mixture turns golden brown and is thoroughly cooked.

- After baking, allow the dish to cool for about 5 minutes before cutting it into slices.

Fromage frais with granola & berries

4 Points

- Preparation Time: 5 min
- Cook Time: 25 min
- Total time: 30 min
- Servings: 4

Ingredients

- Rolled Oats – 25 grams
- Pepitas – 5 grams
- Sunflower Kernels – 5 grams
- Dry Chia Seeds – 5 grams
- Pure Maple Syrup – 2 teaspoons
- Reduced-calorie Coconut Oil Spray – 2 pumps
- Shredded Coconut – 5 grams
- Zero-fat Fruit-Flavored Fromage Frais – 4 medium-sized containers
- Bananas – 4 medium-sized
- Assorted Fresh Berry Mix (naturally sweetened) – 150 grams (includes strawberries, raspberries, and blueberries for garnish)

Preparation Steps

- Warm the oven to 150°C (fan-assisted 130°C, gas mark 2). Prepare a baking sheet with parchment paper.

- Combine the oats and various seeds in a sizable mixing bowl, drizzle with maple syrup, and blend well. Spread this mixture on the prepared sheet, lightly coat with the coconut oil spray, and bake for 20 minutes, stirring now and then. For the last 5 minutes, scatter shredded coconut over the top. Once baked, transfer to a cool tray to cool down.

- Cut the bananas into slices and arrange in serving dishes, alternating with layers of fromage frais. Add a generous helping of the homemade granola and finish with a crown of mixed berries.

Beetroot & egg hash

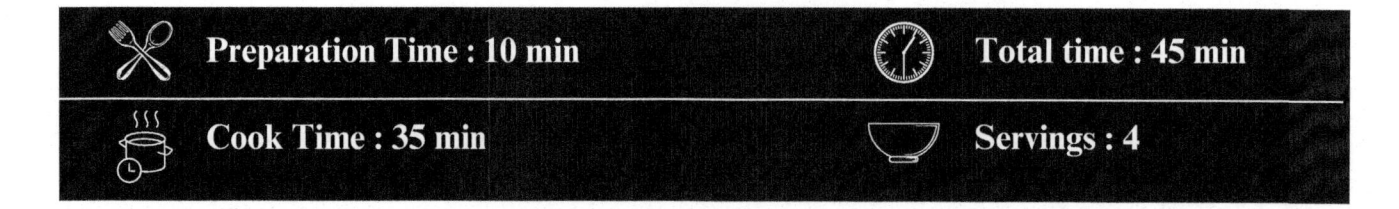

5 Points

Preparation Time : 10 min
Total time : 45 min
Cook Time : 35 min
Servings : 4

Ingredients

- 400 grams of potatoes, peeled and diced
- 4 small beetroots, peeled and diced
- Low-calorie cooking spray, 4 pumps
- 75 grams of chorizo sausage, casing removed and torn into pieces
- 4 medium eggs
- 2 tablespoons of fresh parsley, coarsely chopped

Preparation Steps

- Place potatoes and beetroots in two separate pots and submerge in water. Heat until boiling, then simmer the potatoes for 5 minutes. After draining the potatoes, which should be fork-tender but not fully cooked, continue to simmer the beetroots for an additional 5 minutes. Drain the beetroots, ensuring they have a consistency similar to the potatoes, and allow both to air dry.

- Coat a spacious skillet with the low-calorie cooking spray and warm over medium heat. Introduce the chorizo and sauté for 3 to 4 minutes until the edges are golden and the oils are released. Remove the chorizo using a slotted spoon and set it aside on a plate.

- Into the same skillet, add the potatoes and beetroots, frying them for about 10 minutes until they are evenly browned and soft. Fold the chorizo back into the mixture.

- Create four wells within the hash and gently crack an egg into each. Let them cook for 4 to 5 minutes until the egg

- whites have mostly set. Then cover the skillet for a few more minutes to ensure the whites are fully cooked but the yolks remain runny.

- Garnish the dish with the chopped parsley and season to taste. It is now ready to be served.

Edyth Breese

Egg & bacon roll

6 Points

- Preparation Time : 5 min
- Total time : 15 min
- Cook Time : 10 min
- Servings : 1

Ingredients

- One whole, raw egg
- Two slices of raw bacon medallions
- One large tomato
- One teaspoon of fresh chives
- One medium wholemeal bread roll
- One teaspoon of low-fat mayonnaise

Preparation Steps

- Start by preheating your grill to a moderately high temperature. Commence by placing the egg in a diminutive pot, submerge it completely with cool water, and proceed to boil. Once boiling, reduce the flame marginally and allow the egg to simmer for 8 minutes until it is thoroughly hard-boiled. Following this, drain and refresh the egg with cold tap water. Subsequently, peel the egg and coarsely dice it into a mixing bowl.

- Concurrently, grill the bacon medallions for approximately 1 minute and 30 seconds on each side until cooked. Allow them to cool down before slicing them in half horizontally.

- Incorporate the large tomato, diced, and the majority of the chives into the bowl containing the chopped egg, stirring the mixture. Season the blend with a pinch of salt and freshly ground pepper to taste.

- Bisect the wholemeal bread roll and smear the inside with the low-fat mayonnaise. Arrange the bacon slices on one half and spoon the egg mixture

- over the bacon. Garnish with an additional sprinkle of chives.

- Complete the sandwich by placing the other half of the roll on top. Envelop the sandwich in plastic wrap and refrigerate it until it's time to serve.

Edyth Breese

Cheese & tomato breakfast muffins

5 Points

- Preparation Time : 20 min
- Cook Time : 35 min
- Total time : 55 min
- Servings : 9

Ingredients

- Cooking Spray with Reduced Calories - 4 spritzes
- All-Purpose Flour - 125 grams
- Whole Wheat Flour - 125 grams
- Leavening Agent (Baking Powder) - 2 level teaspoons
- Sodium Bicarbonate (Baking Soda) - ½ level teaspoon
- Low-Fat Margarine - Melt 80 grams
- Fresh Eggs - 2 medium-sized, uncooked
- Partially Skimmed Milk - 200 milliliters
- Reduced-Fat Cheddar - Grate 75 grams
- Fresh Cherry Tomatoes - Chop roughly to get 100 grams
- Fresh Chives - Finely slice to make 1 teaspoon

Preparation Steps

- Start by heating your oven to 190°C (170°C if using a fan oven), which corresponds to gas mark 5. Prepare a muffin tray with 9 liners out of a 12-hole tray.

- Take a sizable mixing bowl and whisk together both types of flour, baking powder, and bicarbonate of soda. Add a pinch of seasoning to taste.

- In a different bowl, whisk the cooled, melted low-fat margarine with the raw eggs, milk, and grated cheese until well combined, then pour this wet mix into the bowl of dry ingredients. Stir thoroughly, then fold in the chopped tomatoes and chives.

- Evenly distribute the batter into the lined muffin cups, and place in the oven to bake for 25-30 minutes, or until the muffins have puffed up and taken on a golden hue.

-

The Weight Watchers Cookbook 2024

Porridge with blueberries

5 Points

Preparation Time : 5 min

Total time : 15 min

Cook Time : 10 min

Servings : 4

Ingredients

- Blueberries (frozen) - 300 grams
- Honey - 1.5 level teaspoons
- Skimmed Milk - 750 milliliters
- Rolled oats - 120 grams

Preparation Steps

- Begin by placing the frozen blueberries into a saucepan, adding two tablespoons of water, along with the honey. Warm the mixture over a medium-low flame for approximately 4 to 5 minutes, gently mashing the blueberries with a wooden spoon as they soften. Once done, remove from heat and set aside.

- In a separate large saucepan, combine the rolled oats and skimmed milk. Bring the mixture to a boil, then lower the heat to allow it to simmer. Continue to cook for another 4 to 5 minutes, stirring consistently, until the mixture reaches a thick, porridge-like consistency.

- Serve the porridge into four individual bowls. Swirl the blueberry mixture into each serving to create a flavorful compote-infused dish ready to enjoy.

Smoked salmon rosti

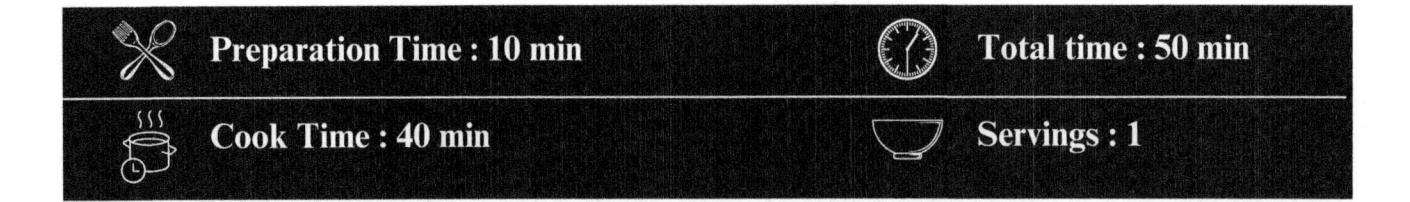

4 Points

- Preparation Time: 10 min
- Cook Time: 40 min
- Total time: 50 min
- Servings: 1

Ingredients

- Low-calorie non-stick cooking spray – 4 applications
- Waxy Charlotte potatoes, peeled - 150 grams
- Small onion, grated
- Natural Greek yogurt, fat-free - 1 heaped tablespoon
- Smoked salmon – 40 grams

Preparation Steps

- Begin by preheating your oven to 190 degrees Celsius with a fan setting of 170 degrees Celsius, or to gas mark 5. Lightly coat a baking tray with the non-stick cooking spray.

- Place the potatoes into a pot of cool water, then raise the heat to achieve a boil. Allow them to simmer for about 5 minutes, or until they are slightly tender yet still firm at the core. Proceed to drain the water.

- Once the potatoes are manageable to touch, grate them into a mixing bowl. Incorporate the grated onion and a small dash of salt, stirring the mixture thoroughly.

- Form the mixture into three evenly sized portions, arrange them on the prepared baking tray, and press down to flatten each one. Apply another light coating of the cooking spray and bake for 30 minutes. Remember to turn them over after 20 minutes to ensure they are crisp and golden brown on both sides.

- To serve, place the rösti on a plate,

adding a dollop of the Greek yogurt on top, followed by the smoked salmon. Finish with a sprinkle of freshly ground black pepper to taste.

French toast crumpets with blueberry compôte

9 Points

Preparation Time : 5 min
Total time : 27 min
Cook Time : 22 min
Servings : 4

Ingredients

- Fresh Blueberries - 300 grams
- Zest of one Lemon
- Medium Eggs (raw) - 4
- Skimmed Milk - 80 milliliters
- Pure Vanilla Extract - 1 leveled teaspoon
- Ground Cinnamon - ½ leveled teaspoon
- Agave Nectar - 2 leveled teaspoons
- Low-calorie Cooking Spray - 4 pumps
- Crumpets - 8 pieces
- Greek Yogurt (non-fat) - 150 grams

Preparation Steps

- Begin by placing the blueberries and lemon zest into a saucepan. Secure the lid and let them simmer for about 10 minutes, or until the blueberries soften and create a thick, jam-like consistency.

- In a separate bowl, vigorously mix the eggs, skimmed milk, vanilla extract, cinnamon, and agave nectar until well combined.

- Submerge each crumpet into the egg mixture, allowing them to soak for approximately 2 minutes.

- Lightly coat a skillet with the low-calorie cooking spray and place it over medium heat. Cook the soaked crumpets in the skillet, doing so in batches if necessary, for about 2 to 3 minutes on each side until they are golden brown.

- Present the warm crumpets accompanied by the homemade blueberry sauce and a dollop of the non-fat Greek yogurt.

The Weight Watchers Cookbook 2024

Lunchtime Delights

Edyth Breese

- Curried butternut Squash soup
- Baked vegetable Frittata
- Mushroom soup
- Roasted veg and tuna salad
- Aubergine pizza slices
- Asian Style Turkey Salad
- Mushroom and ham frittata with potato salad
- Warm Kale and Chicken Salad
- Beef and Paprika soup with Soured cream
- Beetroot and Mackerel toastie
- Mushroom 'pizzas' with wedges
- Roasted Pepper Crumpet Pizza
- Cauliflower, Coconut and Tumeric Soup
- Greek style orto salad

Edyth Breese

The Weight Watchers Cookbook 2024

Curried butternut squash soup

0 Points

- **Preparation Time : 15 min**
- **Cook Time : 55 min**
- **Total time : 1 hr 10 min**
- **Servings : 6**

Ingredients

- Butternut Squash - 800 grams, peeled, seeds removed, chopped into 2.5 cm pieces

- Onion - 2 medium-sized, each cut into quarters

- Vegetable Broth Cube - 2 cubes, dissolved in 2 pints of boiling water

- Curry Spice Blend - 1.5 teaspoons

- Fresh Rosemary - 1 small branch, leaves stripped and finely chopped

- Seasoning - A pinch of salt and freshly ground black pepper, adjusted to taste

Preparation Steps

- Begin by heating your oven to 220°C (fan-assisted 200°C, gas mark 4). Arrange the butternut squash and onion pieces in a spacious roasting tray and roast them without a cover for 45 minutes, or until the squash feels soft when pierced. Move the roasted vegetables to a large pot and pour in the prepared vegetable broth. Bring the mixture to a boil, then lower the heat and let it simmer for 15 minutes. Allow the mixture to cool down for about 15 minutes. Then, working in portions, blend the mixture until smooth using a blender or food processor.

- In a separate pan over low heat, gently toast the curry spice blend for approximately 2 minutes until it exudes a rich aroma, taking care not to let it burn. Blend the toasted spices into the smooth soup mixture. Season the soup with salt and pepper according to your preference.

- Serve the soup, equally distributed into six servings. Embellish each with the finely chopped rosemary. It is best enjoyed warm.

Edyth Breese

Baked vegetable frittata

0 Points

Preparation Time : 15 min **Total time : 50 min**
Cook Time : 35 min **Servings : 6**

Ingredients

- Aubergine - 1 medium-sized, sliced
- Courgette - 1 medium-sized, sliced lengthwise
- Low-calorie cooking spray: 10 sprays
- Onion: 1 medium-sized, finely diced
- Garlic: 1 clove, minced
- Mixed Peppers: 225 grams, roasted and drained (preserved in brine)
- Eggs: 6 medium-sized, whole
- Skim Milk: 4 tablespoons
- Dried Oregano: 2 level teaspoons
- Salt: ¼ teaspoon, or adjust to taste
- Ground Black Pepper: ¼ teaspoon

Preparation Steps

- Start by heating the grill. Place the aubergine and courgette slices on the grill tray and lightly mist with the calorie-controlled cooking spray. Grill for about 3 minutes on each side, or alternatively, use a char-grill pan for cooking them.

- At the same time, coat a non-stick skillet with the cooking spray and sauté the onion and garlic for 3-4 minutes, stirring frequently, then take off the heat. Preheat your oven to Gas Mark 5/190°C/170°C with a fan.

- Prepare a 23cm (9-inch) round baking dish by spraying it with the cooking spray. Create a base layer using half of the eggplant slices and half of the roasted peppers. Add the courgette slices on top, evenly distributing some of the sautéed onion and garlic mixture between layers. Finish by layering the remaining roasted peppers and eggplant slices.

- In a bowl, whisk together the eggs, milk, and dried oregano. Season the mixture with salt and black pepper.

- Evenly pour this mixture over the layered vegetables in the baking dish.

- Place the dish in the preheated oven and bake for 25 minutes, or until the egg mixture is set and the top is a golden brown color. This dish can be served either warm or chilled, cut into wedge-shaped slices.

Mushroom soup

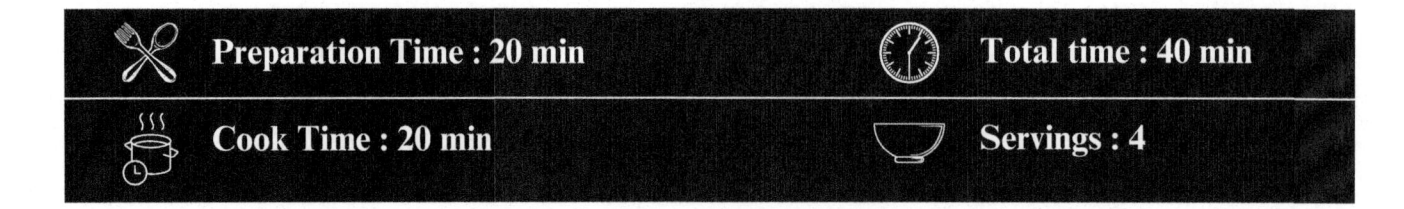

2 Points

- Preparation Time : 20 min
- Cook Time : 20 min
- Total time : 40 min
- Servings : 4

Ingredients

- Extra Virgin Olive Oil - 1 tablespoon
- Finely Chopped Shallots - 125 grams
- Crushed Garlic Cloves - 2
- Dry Sherry - 2 tablespoons
- Sliced Chestnut Mushrooms - 650 grams, reserve 4 whole mushrooms for garnish
- Vegetable Stock Cube - 1 cube (to prepare 750ml of stock)
- Large Can of Cooked Borlotti Beans - Drained and rinsed
- Fresh Rosemary Sprig - 1
- Calorie-Controlled Cooking Spray - 4 sprays
- Greek Yogurt with 0% Fat - 4 tablespoons
- Fresh Parsley Sprigs - 4, for garnishing

Preparation Steps

- Warm the olive oil in a sizable saucepan over moderate heat. Introduce the chopped shallots and sauté for 4 minutes until they soften. Incorporate the crushed garlic and continue stirring for an additional half-minute.

- Pour in the dry sherry and let it simmer for 2 minutes or until it has nearly evaporated.

- Add the sliced mushrooms to the saucepan and stir-fry for about 4 minutes until they turn soft. Introduce the stock, the borlotti beans, and the rosemary sprig, then bring the mixture to a boil. Lower the heat to maintain a gentle simmer and continue cooking for 10 minutes.

- After cooking, remove the rosemary sprig and discard it. Employ a stick blender to puree the mushroom mixture until smooth, creating a creamy soup.

- In parallel, lightly coat a non-stick skillet with the calorie-controlled cooking spray and place it over

- Thinly slice the whole mushrooms reserved for garnish and fry them for 4 minutes.

- Ladle the soup into four individual bowls. Swirl a tablespoon of Greek yogurt into each serving. Crown each bowl with the sautéed mushroom slices and a sprig of fresh parsley.

Edyth Breese

Roasted veg & tuna salad

2 Points

- Preparation Time : 15 min
- Total time : 50 min
- Cook Time : 35 min
- Servings : 4

Ingredients

- Bell Peppers (assorted types) - medium-sized, chopped into pieces
- Courgette, 3 medium-sized - sliced into thick circles
- Red Onions - 2 small, cut into segments
- Rapeseed Oil - 1 tablespoon
- Chickpeas (cooked) - 1 large can, drained
- Fresh Basil - 2 tablespoons, roughly chopped
- Garlic - 1 clove, minced
- Extra Virgin Olive Oil - 1 tablespoon

Preparation Steps

- Start by heating your oven to 200°C (fan-assisted 180°C, gas mark 6).

- Arrange the bell peppers, zucchini, and red onions in a spacious roasting pan and sprinkle with the rapeseed oil. Roast for approximately 30-35 minutes or until they are soft. Once done, remove from the oven and let cool to room temperature before incorporating the drained chickpeas.

- For the dressing, whisk together the chopped basil, minced garlic, extra virgin olive oil, and lemon juice in a separate bowl.

- Pour the dressing over the roasted vegetables, ensuring an even coating, and then gently fold in the spinach leaves.

- Adjust the seasoning according to your preference. Place the mixture on a serving dish and garnish with the drained tuna on top before serving.

The Weight Watchers Cookbook 2024

Aubergine pizza slices

2 Points

- Preparation Time : 10 min
- Cook Time : 20 min
- Total time : 30 min
- Servings : 4

Ingredients

- Aubergine- 3 medium-sized
- Low-calorie Cooking Spray - 4 spritzes
- Onion - 1 small, finely diced
- Garlic - 1 clove, minced
- Fresh Oregano - 1 teaspoon, chopped
- Canned Tomatoes - 1 large can
- Reduced-fat Mozzarella Cheese - 1 piece, roughly shredded
- Fresh Basil Leaves - 6 leaves

Preparation Steps

- Start by preheating your oven to 200°C (fan-assisted 180°C, gas mark 6). Position a wire rack over a baking tray. Cut the aubergine into 8 slices each, about 1.5cm in thickness. Place the slices on the rack and lightly coat with the low-calorie spray. Roast for 12-15 minutes until they turn a nice golden brown, flipping and spraying again midway through the roast time.

- For the sauce, lightly coat a saucepan with the cooking spray and sauté the onion for 3-4 minutes until it begins to soften. Mix in the minced garlic and continue cooking for an additional minute. Add the fresh oregano and canned tomatoes, season to taste, and let it simmer for 10 minutes until the sauce thickens slightly.

- Heat up the grill. After the aubergine are roasted, take them out of the oven and spoon the tomato sauce on each slice. Sprinkle the torn mozzarella and basil leaves on top, setting aside a few leaves for garnish. Grill for 2-3 minutes until the cheese bubbles and turns a golden color.

- Finish by garnishing with the remaining basil leaves before serving.

The Weight Watchers Cookbook 2024

Asian-style Turkey Salad

3 Points

- Preparation Time : 5 min
- Total time : 20 min
- Cook Time : 15 min
- Servings : 4

Ingredients

- Low-calorie cooking spray - 4 pumps
- Skinless roasted turkey - 200 grams, pulled apart
- Five Spice Powder - 1 level teaspoon
- Pure honey - ½ level tablespoon
- Zest of half a lime
- Fresh beansprouts - 2 tablespoons
- Raw carrots - 2 medium-sized, julienned
- Green onions - 3 medium-sized, cleaned and chopped
- Cucumber - ½ medium-sized, julienned
- Halved cherry tomatoes - 150 grams
- Mixed salad greens - 80 grams
- Chopped fresh cilantro - 1 small bunch

Preparation Steps

- Coat a non-stick skillet with the low-calorie cooking spray and sauté the shredded turkey with the Five Spice Powder over medium heat for a few minutes, until the turkey is thoroughly warmed. Stir in the honey and lime zest and continue to cook for an additional 2 minutes. Then, take the skillet off the heat.

- In the meantime, quickly boil the beansprouts in a pot of water for 1 minute. Drain them, cool immediately under cold running water, and transfer to a large mixing bowl.

- Combine the remaining vegetables with the mixed greens, cilantro, and mint in the bowl with the beansprouts. In a separate bowl, whisk together the lime juice, soy sauce, Thai fish sauce, light brown sugar, garlic, and ginger to create the dressing. Drizzle this over the salad and toss everything to ensure an even coating.

- Portion out the salad into individual serving bowls. Top each serving with the warm spiced turkey and a sprinkle of chopped peanuts to serve.

- Chopped fresh mint - 1 small bunch
- Chopped unsalted peanuts - 20 grams
- Freshly squeezed lime juice - 30 milliliters
- Soy sauce - 1 tablespoon
- Thai fish sauce - 1 teaspoon
- Light brown sugar - ½ teaspoon
- Minced garlic - 1 teaspoon
- Minced fresh ginger - 1 teaspoon

The Weight Watchers Cookbook 2024

Mushroom & ham frittata with potato salad

4 Points

Preparation Time : 10 min	Total time : 25 min
Cook Time : 15 min	Servings : 4

Ingredients

- Halved New Potatoes - 400 g
- Fresh Watercress - 100 g
- Sliced Red Onion - ½ of a small one
- Low-Calorie Cooking Spray - 4 sprays
- Sliced Mushrooms - 300 g
- Chopped Honey Roast Ham - 100 g
- Whole Eggs, beaten - 8 medium
- Olive Oil - 2 teaspoons
- Balsamic Vinegar - 1 teaspoon
- Level Dijon Mustard - 1 teaspoon

Preparation Steps

- Preheat your oven to a temperature of 200°C (fan-assisted 180°C, gas mark 6). Boil a pot of water, then add the halved potatoes and let them cook for about 10 minutes until they're soft. Once done, drain them and let them cool in a separate bowl.

- Coat a 25cm non-stick, oven-safe skillet with four sprays of the low-calorie cooking spray. Heat the pan over a medium flame. Toss in the mushrooms and sauté them for approximately 4 to 5 minutes until they're cooked through.

- Introduce the chopped ham and beaten eggs into the pan, stirring for another 2 to 3 minutes until the mixture begins to set. Move the skillet to the preheated oven and allow it to bake for an additional 2 minutes or until the surface turns a golden brown and is fully set.

- In a small bowl, whisk together the olive oil, balsamic vinegar, and Dijon mustard, adding a bit of water to achieve the desired dressing consistency. Season to taste. In a large serving bowl, combine the boiled

- potatoes, watercress, and sliced onion. Pour the prepared dressing over this mixture and toss everything to ensure an even coating.

- Once the frittata is cooked, cut it into wedge-shaped slices. Serve these alongside the dressed potato salad. Enjoy a balanced meal featuring a golden-brown frittata accompanied by a tangy potato salad.

The Weight Watchers Cookbook 2024

Warm kale & chicken salad **5 Points**

Preparation Time : 20 min	Total time : 1 hr 5 min
Cook Time : 45 min	Servings : 4

Ingredients

- Butternut Squash - 800 grams, peeled, cubed (2 cm)//
- Low calorie cooking spray - 4 spritzes
- Red Onion - 1 medium, thinly sliced
- Chicken Breast, Boneless and Skinless - 4 medium pieces
- Chorizo - 80 grams, casings removed
- Breadcrumbs - 25 grams, freshly made
- Extra Virgin Olive Oil - 1.5 tablespoons
- Dijon Mustard - 1 tablespoon, leveled
- Balsamic Vinegar - 1.5 teaspoons
- Kale - 80 grams, baby leaves

Preparation Steps

- Warm the oven to 200°C (fan-assisted 180°C, gas mark 6). Arrange the butternut squash on a baking sheet, lightly coat with the low-calorie cooking spray, and season. Bake for 45 minutes until soft, stirring midway through the cooking time. After 20 minutes, incorporate the sliced red onion.

- Place a grill pan over high heat. Sandwich the chicken breasts between two pieces of plastic wrap and pound them flat with a rolling pin, then lightly coat with cooking spray. Grill each side for 5 minutes or until the chicken is thoroughly cooked. Slice the chicken into generous pieces.

- Use a small food processor to pulse the chorizo into fine crumbs. Over medium heat, cook the chorizo in a non-stick skillet until it begins to exude its oil. Introduce the breadcrumbs and stir for 4-5 minutes until they are golden and crunchy.

- Combine the olive oil, Dijon mustard, and balsamic vinegar in a bowl, adding seasoning to taste. .

- Drizzle this dressing over the kale, roasted squash, and onion, tossing everything to ensure an even coating.

- To serve, distribute the salad among plates, and top with the grilled chicken and the chorizo breadcrumb mix

The Weight Watchers Cookbook 2024

Beef & paprika soup with soured cream

6 Points

- Preparation Time : 15 min
- Cook Time : 1 hr 45 min
- Total time : 2 hrs
- Servings : 4

Ingredients

- Olive Oil - 1 tablespoon, divided

- Lean Beef Stew Meat - 450 grams, with fat removed and chopped into 2-centimeter cubes

- Onion - 1 large, finely chopped

- Carrots - 2 medium-sized, diced

- Celery Stalks - 2, diced

- Garlic Cloves - 2, minced

- Paprika - 1 level tablespoon, with additional for garnish

- Low-Sodium Beef Broth - 750 milliliters, prepared from 1 stock cube

- Canned Tomatoes - 1 large can

- Raw Potatoes - 200 grams, chopped into 2-centimeter pieces

- Spinach - 100 grams

- Light Sour Cream - 2 level tablespoons

Preparation Steps

- Begin by heating half of the olive oil in a substantial pot over a robust flame. Sear the beef for approximately 3 minutes until it achieves an even browning. Remove the beef from the pot and place it aside on a dish.

- Diminish the heat to a moderate level and introduce the remaining oil into the pot. Sauté the onion, carrots, and celery, stirring consistently, for 5 minutes until they exhibit a softened texture. Incorporate the minced garlic and paprika, cooking for an additional minute.

- Reintroduce the browned beef into the pot along with the prepared beef broth, tomatoes, and 250 milliliters of water. Elevate the heat to bring the concoction to a boil, then lower the heat and let it simmer with a cover for 1 hour. Following this, add the potato pieces and continue to simmer without a cover for another 30 minutes or until the potatoes are tender and the beef is succulent and easily pulled apart. Fold in the spinach just until it wilts.

- Serve the hearty soup in individual bowls, each garnished with a dollop of light sour cream and a light dusting of paprika for an additional burst of flavor.

The Weight Watchers Cookbook 2024

Beetroot & mackerel toastie

6 Points

- Preparation Time : 10 min
- Cook Time : 5 min
- Total time : 15 min
- Servings : 2

Ingredients

- Raw Mackerel - 2 medium-sized fillets
- Reduced-Fat Crème Fraîche:m - 75 grams
- Brined Capers - 1 tablespoon, thoroughly rinsed
- Fresh Dill - 1 tablespoon, finely minced, additional for embellishment
- Fresh Lemon Juice - 20 milliliters
- Whole Grain Sandwich Thins - 2 pieces
- Vacuum-Packed Beetroot - 250 grams, sliced into wedges
- Lemon Zest - from half a lemon

Preparation Steps

- Warm the grill to a medium-high setting. Season the mackerel fillets lightly and arrange them on a compact baking sheet.

- Grill for 3 to 4 minutes, or until they are thoroughly cooked. Allow them to cool for a short period, then shred the fish into smaller pieces. While the mackerel is cooling down, blend the reduced-fat crème fraîche with the capers and minced dill, incorporating a dash of fresh lemon juice.

- Separate the sandwich thins and lightly toast them. Layer the beetroot wedges and the shredded mackerel atop the toasted thins. Spoon a generous amount of the crème fraîche blend over the mackerel.

- Finally, adorn with additional dill and sprinkle with lemon zest before serving.

Cauliflower, coconut & turmeric soup

7 Points

Preparation Time : 10 min
Cook Time : 40 min
Total time : 50 min
Servings : 4

Ingredients

- Extra Virgin Olive Oil – 1 tbsp
- Yellow Onion – 1 medium-sized, finely diced
- Garlic Cloves – 2, minced
- Fresh Ginger – 15g, peeled and shredded
- Fresh Chilies (either green or red) – 2, thinly sliced
- Ground Turmeric – 3 tsp
- Fresh Cauliflower – 1 head, segmented into bite-sized florets
- Light Coconut Milk (7.7% Fat) – 1 tin
- Vegetable Bouillon Cube – 1, dissolved in 600 ml of hot water
- Pure Lime Juice – 2 tbsp
- Fresh Cilantro (Coriander) – 2 tbsp, chopped

Preparation Steps

- Begin by warming the olive oil in a sizable saucepan set over a moderate flame. Sauté the chopped onion for approximately 6 to 8 minutes until it becomes translucent and soft. Introduce the minced garlic, shredded ginger, half of the sliced chili peppers, and the ground turmeric to the pan, continuing to stir for an additional 2 minutes.

- Next, incorporate the cauliflower florets into the mixture and continue to sauté for a further 5 minutes. Carefully pour in the coconut milk, setting aside 2 tablespoons for garnishing later, and add the prepared vegetable stock. Allow the mixture to gently simmer for around 25 to 30 minutes, or until you find the cauliflower has softened to your preference.

- Once cooked, remove the pan from the heat source and give it a moment to cool down slightly. Using an immersion blender, blend the contents until you achieve a smooth purée. Blend in the fresh lime juice and adjust the seasoning to suit your taste.

- To serve, ladle the soup into bowls and enhance each serving with a drizzle of the reserved coconut milk, a sprinkle of the remaining sliced chili peppers, and a scattering of fresh cilantro leaves.

Edyth Breese

Mushroom 'pizzas' with wedges

6 Points

- Preparation Time : 15 min
- Total time : 55 min
- Cook Time : 40 min
- Servings : 4

Ingredients

- Low-calorie cooking spray - 4 sprays
- Small red onion - finely diced
- Garlic - 2 cloves, minced
- Canned tomatoes - 2 large cans
- Tomato paste - 1 tablespoon
- Fresh oregano - 2 teaspoons, finely chopped
- Dried bay leaf - 1
- Balsamic vinegar - 1 teaspoon
- Raw potatoes - 600 grams, sliced into wedges
- Smoked paprika, 1 teaspoon
- Large portobello mushrooms - 8, stems removed
- Sliced olives in brine - 50 grams
- Sliced sun-dried tomatoes - 50 grams

Preparation Steps

- Preheat your oven to 200°C (fan-assisted 180°C, gas mark 4). Lightly coat a pan with low-calorie cooking spray and sauté the chopped red onion for about 5 minutes until it softens. Introduce the minced garlic and continue cooking for an additional 2 minutes.

- Stir in the canned tomatoes, tomato paste, chopped oregano, bay leaf, and balsamic vinegar. Add seasoning to taste and let the mixture simmer for 20 minutes, allowing it to thicken.

- In the meantime, arrange the potato wedges in a roasting tray. Apply a light coating of the cooking spray and sprinkle with smoked paprika. Season as desired and mix well. Roast for 35-40 minutes, turning the wedges halfway through the cooking time, until they are crispy.

- Place the portobello mushrooms, gill-side up, on a baking sheet. Distribute the thickened tomato sauce evenly over the mushrooms, and then garnish with the sliced olives, sun-dried tomatoes, and shredded mozzarella cheese.

- Light mozzarella cheese - 125 grams, shredded

- Fresh basil - 1 tablespoon, roughly torn

- Place in the oven to bake with the potato wedges for the last 20 minutes.

- Once finished, remove from the oven and sprinkle the torn basil leaves over the mushrooms. Serve the stuffed mushrooms alongside the crispy potato wedges.

Edyth Breese

Roasted pepper crumpet pizzas

8 Points

Preparation Time : 5 min
Cook Time : 7 min
Total time : 12 min
Servings : 4

Ingredients

- Crumpets - 4
- Pesto Sauce - 1⅓ tablespoons or 4 teaspoons, leveled
- Italian Seasoning Blend - 2 teaspoons
- Sweet Piquanté Peppers - ½ of a 150g jar
- Cherry Tomatoes - 8, sliced in half
- Red Onion - ½ of a small onion
- Fresh Basil Leaves - 4, for decoration

Preparation Steps

- Begin by preheating your oven to 190°C if it's a conventional type, 170°C if it's a fan-assisted model, or set it to gas mark 5.

- Arrange the crumpets on a baking tray. Each crumpet should be evenly coated with 1 teaspoon of pesto sauce, then dusted with the Italian seasoning blend.

- Evenly distribute the sweet piquanté peppers, halved cherry tomatoes, and red onion across the crumpets. Add a touch of black pepper to taste.

- Allow them to bake in the preheated oven for a duration of 6 to 7 minutes.

- Once baked, present the crumpets with a garnishing of fresh basil leaves.

The Weight Watchers Cookbook 2024

Greek-style orzo salad

10 Points

Preparation Time : 5 min **Total time : 17 min**

Cook Time : 12 min **Servings : 4**

Ingredients

- Orzo Pasta, uncooked - 280 grams
- Fresh Cherry Tomatoes - 200 grams, sliced in halves
- Medium Cucumber - 1 unit, chopped
- Black Olives, without pits - 50 grams, preserved in brine
- Extra Virgin Olive Oil - 1 tablespoon
- Lemon - 1 tablespoon of juice and zest
- Feta Cheese, reduced-fat - 75 grams, crumbled

Preparation Steps

- Begin by boiling the orzo pasta in a pot of salted water for approximately 10 to 12 minutes, or until it reaches an al dente texture. Once cooked, drain the pasta and rinse it with cold water to lower its temperature. Drain once more and place it into a mixing bowl. Add the halved cherry tomatoes, diced cucumber, and black olives to the bowl.

- In a separate container, combine extra virgin olive oil with freshly grated lemon zest and juice. Season the mixture to taste. Drizzle this homemade dressing over the pasta mixture and toss thoroughly to ensure all ingredients are evenly coated.

- To finish, sprinkle the crumbled light feta cheese over the top of the salad. The dish is now ready to be served.

Edyth Breese

The Weight Watchers Cookbook 2024

Dinner Feasts

Edyth Breese

- Chicken Lentil and Kale Braise
- Mustard Glaze Salmons with Lentils
- Prosciutto-wrapped haddock with celeriac mash
- Boodles with Harissa meatballs
- Tofu pho
- Mushroom & Spinach Spaghetti
- India Style vegetable Stir-fry
- Griddled rump steak with Chios & Mustard Mayo
- Gluten-free beef Lasagne
- French Onion Risotto
- Lentil Bolognese & sweet potato
- Prawn Singapore noodles

Edyth Breese

The Weight Watchers Cookbook 2024

Chicken, lentil & kale braise

0 Points

- Preparation Time : 5 min
- Total time : 20 min
- Cook Time : 15 min
- Servings : 4

Ingredients

- Low-calorie nonstick cooking spray - 4 spritzes
- Skinless raw chicken breast fillets - 500 g, mini
- Fresh thyme - 1 tablespoon, preferably lemon thyme, finely chopped
- Medium red bell pepper - 1, coarsely chopped
- Garlic cloves - 2, thinly sliced
- Raw kale - 200 g, coarsely chopped
- Cooked green or brown lentils - 1 large can, thoroughly drained and rinsed
- Freshly squeezed lemon juice - 4 tablespoons
- Raw corn on the cob - 4 medium-sized ears

Preparation Steps

- Lightly coat a nonstick skillet with the low-calorie cooking spray and warm it over medium-high heat. Introduce the chicken mini fillets and the chopped lemon thyme, cooking and occasionally turning them for about 5 minutes or until they start to brown. Once done, transfer the chicken to a plate and keep it aside.

- Apply another layer of cooking spray to the skillet, then add the chopped red bell pepper and sliced garlic. Sauté for 4 minutes until they soften. Incorporate the chopped kale, stirring for an additional minute, before mixing in the cooked lentils and the lemon juice.

- Place the chicken fillets back into the skillet, arranging them over the lentil and kale mixture. Cover the skillet and let it cook for 3 minutes, or until the chicken is thoroughly cooked. In the meantime, prepare the corn on the cob in the microwave according to the package instructions.

- To serve, present the chicken atop the lentil and kale mixture with the corn on the cob as an accompaniment.

Mustard glazed salmon with lentils

3 Points

- Preparation Time : 5 min
- Cook Time : 20 min
- Total time : 25 min
- Servings : 4

Ingredients

- Extra Virgin Olive Oil - 1 and a half tablespoons
- Red Onions - 2 medium-sized, thinly sliced
- Pure Honey - 1 level teaspoon
- Balsamic Vinegar - 3 teaspoons
- Cooked Green or Brown Lentils - 2 large cans, drained
- Fine Smooth Mustard: 2 level teaspoons
- Raw Salmon Fillets - 4 medium-sized pieces
- Fresh Arugula - 80 grams
- Freshly Squeezed Lemon Juice - 25 milliliters

Preparation Steps

- Begin by preheating your oven to 200°C (fan-assisted 180°C, gas mark 6) and prepare a baking tray with parchment paper.

- In a sizable skillet, warm up 1 tablespoon of olive oil over a gentle flame. Sauté the sliced onions for 8-10 minutes until they have softened considerably.

- Introduce the honey and balsamic vinegar to the pan, continuing to cook for an additional 5-6 minutes until the mixture takes on a caramelized texture. Fold in the lentils and heat them up for a few more minutes, then remove from the stove and set aside to stay warm.

- In a separate container, whisk together the mustard, lemon juice, and the remaining olive oil to create a dressing.

- Arrange the salmon fillets on the lined baking tray. Season to taste and then lavish them with the prepared dressing. Allow them to roast in the oven for about 12 minutes, or until they are thoroughly cooked.

- To finish, incorporate the arugula into the warm lentil mixture and serve alongside the roasted salmon fillets.

Prosciutto-wrapped haddock with celeriac mash

3 Points

- Preparation Time : 5 min
- Total time : 30 min
- Cook Time : 25 min
- Servings : 4

Ingredients

- Celeriac (uncooked) - 800 grams, chopped into chunks of 2-3 cm
- Haddock (uncooked) - 4 medium-sized fillets
- Prosciutto - 8 slices
- Cherry Tomatoes - 250 grams
- Reduced-Fat Crème Fraîche - 1.5 level tablespoons
- Young Spinach Leaves - 400 grams
- Lemon - 1 medium-sized, sliced into wedges for serving

Preparation Steps

- Begin by heating your oven to a temperature of 200°C (or 180°C with a fan), equivalent to gas mark 6. In a sizable pot, bring water to a rolling boil. Add the celeriac pieces and let them simmer for about 20 minutes, or until they become soft. After draining the celeriac, place it back into the pot and allow it to sit for an additional 5 minutes to dry out. Add seasoning to taste and blend in the crème fraîche to create a smooth mash.

- In the meantime, take each haddock fillet and carefully wrap it with a slice of prosciutto. Arrange the wrapped fillets onto a baking sheet along with the cherry tomatoes. Place in the oven to cook for approximately 10-12 minutes. The dish is ready when the prosciutto has taken on a golden hue and the haddock is thoroughly cooked.

- To prepare the spinach, use a large non-stick skillet or frying pan. Add the spinach with a small amount of water and cook until the leaves have wilted. Ensure you season it generously.

- To plate, evenly distribute the celeriac mash onto the plates, and gently place a prosciutto-wrapped haddock fillet on top of each. Accompany the dish with the baked cherry tomatoes and wilted spinach. Garnish with lemon wedges to add a fresh citrus flavor upon serving.

Boodles with harissa meatballs

5 Points

Preparation Time : 20 min
Total time : 45 min
Cook Time : 25 min
Servings : 4

Ingredients

- Low-Calorie Cooking Spray -4 sprays
- Diced Red Onion - 1 medium-sized
- Lean Ground Beef (5% fat) -500 grams
- Harissa Seasoning - 40 grams
- Cumin Powder - 1 level teaspoon
- Fresh Coriander (Cilantro) - 2 tablespoons, chopped
- Ground Coriander - 1 level teaspoon
- Minced Garlic - 2 cloves
- Whole Cherry Tomatoes in Juice - 2 large cans
- Fresh Baby Spinach - 200 grams
- Reduced-Fat Feta Cheese - 50 grams, crumbled

Preparation Steps

- Lightly coat a small pan with the low-calorie cooking spray and gently sauté the diced red onion over medium heat for 8-10 minutes until it's tender. Once done, place the onions on a plate to cool down.

- In a bowl, mix together the ground beef, half of the harissa seasoning, cumin powder, both fresh and dried coriander, minced garlic, and the sautéed onions. Season to taste and form the mixture into 12 evenly sized balls.

- Using a large non-stick skillet coated with cooking spray and set to medium heat, sear the meatballs until they're evenly browned. Add the cherry tomatoes along with the remaining harissa seasoning and let it simmer for 10 minutes, or until the meatballs are fully cooked and the sauce has reduced to a thicker consistency. Toss in the baby spinach and stir until it just begins to wilt.

- In a separate non-stick skillet also coated with cooking spray, cook the spiralized butternut squash over

- Spiralized Butternut Squash - 600 grams

- medium heat for about 6-7 minutes, or until it's soft.

- To serve, distribute the butternut squash noodles onto plates, place the meatballs on top, and finish by sprinkling crumbled feta cheese over each serving.

Tofu Pho

5 Points

- Preparation Time: 10 min
- Cook Time: 45 min
- Total time: 55 min
- Servings: 4

Ingredients

- Tofu, plain - 396g
- Hoisin sauce - 2 tbsp
- Soy sauce - 3 tbsp, divided
- Rice wine vinegar - 1 tbsp
- Cooking spray, low-calorie - 4 sprays
- Garlic cloves - 3
- Fresh ginger - 2-inch piece
- Onion, large - 1
- Vegetable stock cubes - 3
- Miso paste - 1 tbsp
- Rice noodles, uncooked -100g
- Courgette, medium - 1
- Pak choi -2 portions
- Sesame seeds - 1 tsp

Preparation Steps

- Begin by wrapping the tofu in paper towels and setting it between two plates. Place a heavy can on top to apply pressure and leave it for a minimum of 30 minutes to extract excess water. Afterwards, discard the drained liquid and slice the tofu into 12 pieces.

- In a small bowl, whisk together the hoisin sauce, 1 tablespoon of soy sauce, and rice wine vinegar. Lay the tofu slices in a flat dish and drench them with the marinade. Allow them to soak for 20 minutes.

- Heat a large pot over medium-high heat and mist it with low-calorie cooking spray. Introduce the garlic, ginger, and onion to the pot, sautéing for 6 to 8 minutes until they develop a charred appearance, stirring now and then.

- Pour two scoops of vegetable broth into the pot to loosen any bits stuck to the bottom, anticipating a vigorous sizzle. Incorporate the remaining broth and the rest of the soy sauce. Let the mixture come to a gentle boil, then turn

- down the heat, cover the pot, and let it simmer for 30 minutes. Following this, filter the broth and reintegrate it into the pot with the miso paste.

- While the broth simmers, cook the tofu by heating a grill pan over medium-high heat and coating it with cooking spray. Grill the tofu for 3 minutes on each side until grill marks appear. In the meantime, submerge the rice noodles in boiling water for 4 minutes, then drain and place them in cold water.

- Reheat the broth to a simmer and add the pak choi, allowing it to cook for 3 minutes until it's slightly wilted. Incorporate the courgette and noodles, cooking everything for an additional minute.

- Divide the vegetables and noodles evenly among four bowls. Ladle the hot broth over them, then place the grilled tofu on top. Garnish with a sprinkle of sesame seeds before serving.

Mushroom & spinach spaghetti

6 Points

- Preparation Time: 5 min
- Cook Time: 25 min
- Total time: 30 min
- Servings: 4

Ingredients

- Low-Calorie Cooking Spray – 4 sprays
- Red Onion – 1 medium, finely diced
- Garlic – 2 cloves, minced
- Assorted Mushrooms – 800 g (such as chestnut, shiitake, and portobello), slice the larger ones
- Vegetable Broth Cube – 1 cube, used to prepare 300 ml of broth
- Reduced-Fat Cream Cheese – 30 g
- Cornstarch – 2 level teaspoons
- Whole Grain Pasta – 200 g, uncooked spaghetti
- Fresh Spinach – 120 g, baby leaves

Preparation Steps

- Coat a spacious skillet with the low-calorie cooking spray and set it over a medium-high flame. Sauté the chopped red onion for about 4 to 5 minutes until it softens. Incorporate the minced garlic and cook for an additional minute. Introduce the assorted mushrooms to the pan and continue to cook for another 4 to 5 minutes until they turn golden. Pour in the prepared vegetable broth.

- Allow the mixture to simmer for approximately 10 minutes, or until you notice the sauce slightly reducing. Blend in the reduced-fat cream cheese. In a separate bowl, whisk the cornstarch with 2 teaspoons of cold water to create a smooth mixture, then fold this into the sauce. Cook for an additional 3 to 4 minutes until the sauce achieves a thick and lustrous consistency.

- In the meantime, prepare the whole grain pasta according to the package instructions. Once cooked, drain and combine it with the mushroom sauce, adding the fresh spinach. Stir the mixture until the spinach has wilted.

- Season the dish according to your preference, and it's ready to be served.

Edyth Breese

Indian-style vegetable stir-fry

9 Points

- Preparation Time : 5 min
- Total time : 25 min
- Cook Time : 20 min
- Servings : 4

Ingredients

- 600 grams of cauliflower, segmented into florets
- 1 tablespoon of vegetable oil
- 1 tablespoon of mustard seeds, leveled
- 1 medium-sized red onion, sectioned into wedges
- 6 grams of fresh curry leaves, approximately 6 leaves
- 1 teaspoon of chili flakes, leveled
- 2 teaspoons of cumin seeds, leveled
- 1 large can of cooked chickpeas, drained and rinsed
- 1½ teaspoons of turmeric powder
- 250 grams of green beans, ends removed and sliced in half
- 45 milliliters of freshly squeezed lemon juice

Preparation Steps

- Preheat a wok with a lid or a sizable skillet over high heat. Introduce the cauliflower along with 60 milliliters of water. Partially cover and cook for 3 to 4 minutes. Remove the cauliflower from the wok and keep aside.

- Pour the vegetable oil into the wok and sauté the mustard seeds for a minute or until they begin to burst. Incorporate the onion, curry leaves, chili flakes, and cumin seeds, and continue stir-frying for another 5 minutes. Reintroduce the cauliflower to the wok, followed by the chickpeas and turmeric. Stir-fry for an additional 5 minutes.

- Add the green beans and 2½ tablespoons of the lemon juice, adjusting seasoning as needed. Stir-fry for another 3 minutes or until the vegetables are cooked to the desired tenderness.

- In the meantime, apply a light coat of the cooking spray to a small frypan. Over medium-high heat, sear the paneer cubes for 1 minute on each side or until they take on a golden hue.

- 4 spritzes of low-calorie cooking spray

- 200 grams of paneer cheese, cut into cubes

- 1 medium-sized lemon, cut into wedges for serving

- Season with black pepper and drizzle with the remaining lemon juice.

- Present the stir-fried vegetables and golden paneer accompanied by the lemon wedges.

Edyth Breese

Griddled rump steak with chips & mustard mayo

10 Points

Preparation Time : 15 min
Total time : 50 min
Cook Time : 35 min
Servings : 6

Ingredients

- Butternut Squash Fries - 450 grams, sliced into thin fries (skin optional)

- Sweet Potato Fries - 450 grams, thoroughly washed and sliced into thin fries

- Potato Fries - 450 grams, thoroughly washed and sliced into thin fries

- Low-Calorie Cooking Spray - 4 spritzes

- Ground Oregano - 1.5 teaspoons, level

- Lean Rump Steak - 6 medium-sized pieces (225 grams each)

- Fresh Garlic - 6 cloves

- Green Beans - 480 grams

- Fat-Free Greek Yogurt - 300 grams

- Smooth Dijon Mustard - 1.5 teaspoons, level

Preparation Steps

- Preheat your oven to 200°C (fan-assisted 180°C, gas mark 6). Spread the fries out on a large baking sheet in a single layer, lightly coat with the cooking spray, and sprinkle with oregano. Bake for 35 minutes until they are crisp and a golden color, shaking the sheet occasionally to ensure they don't stick.

- For the mustard 'mayo,' whisk together the Greek yogurt, mustard, and lemon juice in a mixing bowl. Adjust seasoning according to your preference.

- Prepare the steaks by seasoning them and adding the garlic on top. Apply a light coating of cooking spray. Place a large griddle pan on high heat and sear the steaks for 2 minutes on each side if you prefer them rare, 3 minutes on each side for medium, and 4 minutes on each side for well-done. After searing, remove the steaks from the pan, cover them with foil, and let them rest for 4-5 minutes.

- Boil the green beans for 4-5 minutes in a pot of water until they are tender. Once cooked, drain the water.

- Freshly Squeezed Lemon Juice - 1.5 tablespoons

- To serve, plate the garlic-infused steaks alongside the fries and green beans. Accompany with the homemade mustard 'mayo'.

Edyth Breese

Gluten-free beef lasagne

11 Points

- Preparation Time : 20 min
- Total time : 1 hr 25 min
- Cook Time : 1 hr 5 min
- Servings : 4

Ingredients

- One medium onion, finely chopped
- Two stalks of celery, diced
- 400 grams of extra lean ground beef (5% fat content), uncooked
- Two medium carrots, diced
- One large can of diced tomatoes
- One beef stock cube, fully dissolved in 200 milliliters of water (verify that it's gluten-free)
- One teaspoon of dried oregano or mixed herbs, leveled
- 300 milliliters of skimmed milk
- One tablespoon of cornflour, leveled
- 100 grams of reduced-fat Cheddar cheese, shredded
- 120 grams of gluten-free lasagne noodles, uncooked

Preparation Steps

- Coat a sizable pan with low-calorie cooking spray and warm it over medium heat. Introduce the chopped onion, diced celery, and ground beef into the pan. Sauté for five minutes, breaking apart the beef until it is thoroughly browned.

- Incorporate the diced carrots, canned tomatoes, prepared beef stock, and oregano. Stir the mixture thoroughly and bring to a boil. Once boiling, reduce the heat, cover the pan, and allow it to simmer for 20 minutes.

- While the meat sauce simmers, preheat your oven to 150°C with a fan, or 170°C without a fan, or gas mark 2.

- For the sauce, mix one tablespoon of milk with the cornflour in a separate bowl and set aside. Heat the remaining milk until just boiling, then lower the heat and blend in the cornflour mixture, stirring continuously until the sauce thickens. Remove from the heat and mix in half of the shredded cheese.

- In a baking dish, layer one-third of the meat sauce at the bottom, followed by

- Four servings of mixed salad greens for accompaniment

- a layer of lasagne noodles. Repeat the layering process, finishing with a final layer of meat sauce. Pour the thickened sauce over the assembled layers and scatter the remaining cheese on top.

- Bake in the preheated oven for approximately 40 minutes, or until the dish is hot and bubbling. Serve hot, accompanied by a fresh green salad.

Edyth Breese

French onion risotto

10 Points

Preparation Time : 10 min **Total time : 1 hr 5 min**
Cook Time : 55 min **Servings : 4**

Ingredients

- Low-calorie cooking spray - 4 spritzes
- Onions - 3 large, thinly sliced
- Garlic - 1 clove, minced
- Arborio rice - 250 grams, uncooked
- Vegetable bouillon cubes - 1.5 cubes, to prepare 1.2 liters of hot broth
- Vegetarian hard cheese, similar to Parmesan - 2 tablespoons, grated
- Fresh parsley - 1 tablespoon, chopped, additional for garnish

Preparation Steps

- Begin by lightly coating a sizeable saucepan with the low-calorie cooking spray. Over a medium flame, sauté the onions for 5 minutes. Continue cooking for an additional 20-25 minutes with the lid on, stirring now and then, until the onions turn a deep golden color. Introduce the minced garlic and continue to cook for one more minute.

- Set aside half of the caramelized onions. Introduce the dry Arborio rice to the saucepan, mixing it with the onions that remain, and sauté for 2 minutes. Prepare 1.2 liters of hot vegetable broth by dissolving 1.5 bouillon cubes in hot water.

- Pour a scoop of the hot broth into the saucepan, stirring occasionally, allowing the rice to absorb the liquid before adding more. Continue this process until all the broth has been incorporated and the rice achieves a tender texture, which should take around 20 minutes.

- Fold in the majority of the grated cheese, the freshly chopped parsley, and the onions you had set aside earlier

- Adjust the seasoning to your preference. Garnish with additional chopped parsley, the rest of the cheese, and a sprinkle of fresh ground black pepper before serving.

Edyth Breese

Lentil Bolognese & sweet potato

5 Points

Preparation Time : 15 min

Cook Time : 1 hr

Total time : 1 hr 15 min

Servings : 4

Ingredients

- Extra Virgin Olive Oil - 1 tablespoon
- Low-Calorie Cooking Spray - 4 pumps
- Fresh Garlic - 2 cloves, minced
- Red Onion - 1 small, diced
- Celery - 1 stalk, diced
- Carrots: 1 medium, diced
- Coriander Seeds - 1 teaspoon, ground
- Cinnamon Powder - ½ teaspoon
- Cooked Green or Brown Lentils: 200 grams
- Canned Chopped Tomatoes - 1 large can
- Vegetable Bouillon Cube - 1 cube, dissolved in 1000ml boiling water
- Fresh Parsley: 1 handful, coarsely chopped

Preparation Steps

- Begin by heating a sizable pan on a medium flame and mist it with the low-calorie cooking spray. Introduce the minced garlic, diced onion, celery, carrot, and the blend of spices, sautéing for about 5 minutes or until the vegetables are slightly softened.

- Proceed to incorporate the cooked lentils, canned tomatoes, and the prepared vegetable broth, stirring the mixture well. Allow the contents to reach a gentle simmer and let it cook for 40 minutes. The goal is for the liquid to reduce and for the lentils to become tender while retaining their shape. Should the lentils require additional cooking time, simply add more water as needed and continue to simmer. Season the mixture to taste and fold in the chopped parsley towards the end.

- In the meantime, warm the reserved olive oil in a separate large frying pan and cook the spiralized sweet potato until it achieves a tender texture. Depending on the size of your pan, you might need to do this in several batches.

- Raw Sweet Potato - 450 grams, peeled and spiralized
- To serve, distribute the cooked sweet potato spirals among the plates and spoon the lentil sauce over them. Finish the dish with a seasoning of freshly ground black pepper to taste.

Edyth Breese

Prawn Singapore noodles

5 Points

Preparation Time : 15 min
Cook Time : 1 hr
Total time : 1 hr 15 min
Servings : 4

Ingredients

- Low-calorie cooking spray - 4 spritzes
- Whole eggs, uncooked - 3 of medium size
- Garlic - 2 cloves, thinly sliced
- Curry powder - 1 tablespoon
- Raw king prawns - 300 grams
- Mixed vegetables for stir-frying - 325 grams
- Dry rice noodles - 250 grams
- Soy sauce - 2 tablespoons
- Thai fish sauce - 2 teaspoons
- Sesame oil - 2 teaspoons

Preparation Steps

- Coat a wok or a sizable skillet with the low-calorie cooking spray and heat it over a medium-high setting. Introduce the eggs and let them cook for about 10 seconds, then scramble until they're fully cooked. Remove the cooked eggs from the pan and place them aside.

- Apply another round of cooking spray to the wok and sauté the garlic slices for 2 to 3 minutes. Incorporate the curry powder and raw prawns and continue to stir-fry for an additional minute. Proceed to add the mixed vegetables and cook for another 5 to 6 minutes, or until they reach your desired level of doneness.

- While the vegetables are cooking, prepare the rice noodles according to the instructions on the package. Once cooked, drain them and then combine the noodles with the set-aside eggs, vegetables, and prawns in the wok.

- In a separate small container, blend the soy sauce, Thai fish sauce, and sesame oil. Drizzle this mixture over the contents of the wok. Stir everything together and cook for one more minute

- to ensure all ingredients are heated through.

- Serve the dish immediately after preparation.

The Weight Watchers Cookbook 2024

Delectable Desserts

Edyth Breese

- Strawberry ripple mouse cake
- Mini Strawberry cheesecakes
- Chai Shortbread
- Spiced Satsuma roulade
- Banana and walnut loaf
- Red velvet cupcakes
- Apricot, blueberry and nit crumble
- Cheats trifle
- Plum Amaretto pudding
- Toffee apple pie
- Steamed lemon pudding
- Apple and Rhubarb crumble
- Cranachan

Edyth Breese

Strawberry ripple mousse cake

3 Points

- Preparation Time : 25 min
- Cook Time : 10 min
- Total time : 35 min
- Servings : 6

Ingredients

- Low-calorie oil spray - 4 spritzes
- Fresh strawberries - 500 grams, topped and sliced vertically
- Agave nectar - 2 tablespoons, leveled
- Pure vanilla extract - ½ teaspoon, leveled
- Premium gelatine leaves - 3 pieces
- Raw egg whites - from 2 eggs
- Superfine sugar - 30 grams
- Natural Greek yogurt, non-fat - 400 grams
- Fresh mint leaves - 10 sprigs, a modest bunch, with leaves separated for garnish

Preparation Steps

- Prepare an 18 cm springform pan by coating it with a low-calorie oil spray and lining it with parchment paper.

- Puree 400 grams of strawberries with agave nectar and vanilla in a food processor until smooth. Strain the mixture to remove seeds and pulp, then set aside one-third of the puree in the refrigerator.

- Soften the gelatine leaves by immersing them in cold water for 5 minutes. Concurrently, warm the remainder of the strawberry puree in a saucepan over medium heat until it begins to bubble; then remove from heat. Drain the gelatine leaves and incorporate them into the warm strawberry puree until fully dissolved. Allow the mixture to cool slightly.

- In a separate bowl, beat the egg whites to stiff peaks, then add the superfine sugar and beat until the mixture is thick and lustrous. Gently fold in the Greek yogurt and the cooled strawberry mixture in increments until well blended.

The Weight Watchers Cookbook 2024

- Position the leftover strawberry slices around the inside edge of the prepared pan, standing upright to create a border. Carefully pour the yogurt mixture into the center, then drizzle the chilled strawberry puree on top and create a marbled effect by swirling with a skewer or knife tip.

- Refrigerate the dessert for at least 4 hours or until set. To serve, release the cake from the pan, remove the parchment, and garnish with the remaining strawberry puree and fresh mint leaves.

The Weight Watchers Cookbook 2024

Mini strawberry cheesecakes

4 Points

- Preparation Time : 5 min
- Total time : 15 min
- Cook Time : 10 min
- Servings : 4

Ingredients

- Crumbled Ginger Nut Cookies - 2 cookies, finely crushed
- Pure Coconut Oil - 1 teaspoon
- Semi-Skimmed Cream Cheese - 70 grams
- Plain Fat-Free Quark - 80 grams
- Fresh Strawberries - 40 grams, ripe, with 4 additional berries for garnish
- Powdered Sugar - 4 teaspoons, sifted
- Pure Vanilla Extract - ¼ teaspoon
- Lemon Zest - From half a lemon

Preparation Steps

- Begin by combining the crushed ginger nut cookies with the coconut oil in a bowl. Evenly distribute this mixture into four individual serving glasses. Use the back of a teaspoon to compress the mixture, creating a solid layer at the bottom of each glass. Place these in the refrigerator to cool as you prepare the filling.

- In a mixing bowl, thoroughly blend the cream cheese with the quark until you achieve a creamy consistency. In a separate dish, mash the ripe strawberries with a fork. Stir one-third of the mashed strawberries into the cream cheese and quark blend. Add the powdered sugar, vanilla extract, and lemon zest to the mixture. Gently fold the remaining strawberry puree into the mixture, creating a marbled effect.Spoon the filling into the chilled glasses, over the ginger nut base. Crown each serving with a whole strawberry for a decorative touch.

- Arrange the glasses on a tray and refrigerate them for a minimum of two hours to allow the dessert to firm up. Serve chilled for a delightful treat.

Chai shortbread

4 Points

- Preparation Time : 15 min
- Total time : 15 min
- Cook Time : 15 min
- Servings : 6

Ingredients

- All-Purpose Flour - 140 grams, with additional for surface dusting

- Gluten-Free Brown Rice Flour (Doves Farm brand recommended) - 40 grams

- Reduced-Fat Margarine - 140 grams, ensure it's at room temperature for ease of use

- Fine Granulated Sugar - 50 grams

- Cardamom: 1 teaspoon of seeds, equivalent to seeds from 6 pods, finely crushed

- Ground Cinnamon - ¾ teaspoon, make sure it's levelled

- Cloves: ¼ teaspoon, levelled, use ground cloves

- Ground Nutmeg - ½ teaspoon, levelled

- Powdered Sugar - 6 teaspoons, levelled

Preparation Steps

- Begin by placing both types of flour and the softened reduced-fat margarine into a small mixing bowl. Using your fingers, blend them together until the mixture takes on a crumbly texture similar to breadcrumbs. Incorporate the granulated sugar and all the spices until evenly mixed.

- Transfer the crumbly mixture onto a surface dusted with flour. Knead the mixture delicately until it forms a cohesive dough. Roll out the dough with a rolling pin to a thickness of about 3-4mm. With a 9cm floral biscuit cutter (or a cutter of a similar shape), cut out 16 shapes. Then, use a 3cm round cutter to create a central hole in each biscuit. Re-roll any leftover dough to use it all up.

- Arrange the shaped biscuits on a large baking tray lined with parchment paper. Place the tray in the refrigerator for 30 minutes to firm up the dough. Meanwhile, preheat your oven to 200°C (fan-assisted 180°C, gas mark 6). Once chilled, bake the biscuits in the preheated oven for 15-18 minutes, or until they're nicely golden.

- Afterwards, transfer them to a wire rack to cool down completely.

- For the icing, blend the powdered sugar with cinnamon, half a tablespoon of water, and an optional 1-2 drops of yellow food coloring until smooth. Drizzle the icing over the cooled biscuits or dip the tops into the icing. Place the biscuits back on the wire rack to allow the icing to set before serving

Edyth Breese

Spiced satsuma roulade

5 Points

Preparation Time : 35 min
Total time : 47 min
Cook Time : 12 min
Servings : 10

Ingredients

- Raw whole eggs - 3 medium-sized
- Fine sugar - 85 grams
- All-purpose flour - 85 grams
- Baking powder - 1 level teaspoon
- Ground cinnamon - 2 level teaspoons
- Satsuma oranges - 600 grams
- Regular sugar - 6 teaspoons
- Additional ground cinnamon - 1 level teaspoon
- Greek yogurt (non-fat) - 500 grams
- Pomegranate seeds - 50 grams
- Powdered sugar - 1 level teaspoon

Preparation Steps

- Heat your oven to a temperature of 200°C (392°F) for a conventional setting, 180°C (356°F) if using a fan-assisted mode, or gas mark 6. Prepare a Swiss roll pan measuring 30 x 24 cm by lining it with parchment paper.

- In a sizable mixing bowl, whisk the eggs and fine sugar with an electric mixer until the mixture is voluminous and retains its form when the whisk is raised. Carefully fold in the all-purpose flour, baking powder, and ground cinnamon, ensuring not to overmix.

- Distribute the batter evenly in the lined pan and smooth the surface. Bake for 12 minutes until the cake turns a golden color and feels springy upon touch. Spread out a piece of parchment paper on a flat surface, identical in size to the cake, and evenly sprinkle 1 teaspoon of regular sugar on it.

- Once the cake is done, invert it onto the sugared parchment paper. Remove the pan and gently peel off the parchment paper that was on top. While the sponge is still warm, roll it up using the bottom sheet of parchment paper to

- assist in forming a tight spiral. Leave it to cool down completely.

- For the filling and garnish, extract juice from half the satsuma oranges into a saucepan. Combine this juice with 6 teaspoons of sugar and a stick of cinnamon and warm over low heat until the sugar dissolves. Turn up the heat to bring the mixture to a boil, then lower the heat and let it simmer until it becomes a thick syrup. Segment the rest of the satsumas, removing any pith, and add them to the syrup. Cook for an additional 3 minutes, then set aside to cool. Remove and discard the cinnamon stick.

- Carefully unroll the roulade and evenly spread the Greek yogurt on top. Chop two-thirds of the satsuma segments roughly and sprinkle them over the yogurt. Re-roll the sponge tightly with the help of the parchment paper.

- Place the roulade seam-side down on a serving dish. Adorn with the remaining satsuma segments and sprinkle pomegranate seeds on top. Just before serving, dust the roulade with powdered sugar.

Banana & walnut loaf

4 Points

- Preparation Time : 40 min
- Total time : 50 min
- Cook Time : 10 min
- Servings : 8

Ingredients

- Low-calorie cooking spray - 4 sprays
- Whole wheat flour - 200g
- Cinnamon powder - 2 level teaspoons
- Chopped walnuts - 20g
- Eggs - 2 medium, raw
- Pure maple syrup - 3 tablespoons
- Bananas - 3 medium, very ripe, mashed, plus 1 sliced lengthwise for garnish

Preparation Steps

- Preheat your oven to 190°C (170°C for fan ovens), equivalent to gas mark 5. Prepare a 450g loaf pan by spraying it with the low-calorie cooking spray and lining it with parchment paper.

- In a sizable bowl, sieve the whole wheat flour and cinnamon together, then mix in the chopped walnuts. In a separate container, beat the eggs. Incorporate the maple syrup and mashed bananas, whisking until well blended.

- Combine the wet ingredients with the dry ingredients in the bowl, folding them gently to ensure the batter is just mixed and not overworked.

- Transfer the batter into the loaf pan you've prepared. Place the banana slices on top of the batter, cut-side facing up, and bake for 40 minutes or until an inserted skewer comes out clean.

- After baking, let the loaf cool in the pan for a short time. Then, remove it from the pan and let it cool completely on a wire rack.

The Weight Watchers Cookbook 2024

Red velvet cupcakes

6 Points

- Preparation Time : 20 min
- Cook Time : 20 min
- Total time : 40 min
- Servings : 12

Ingredients

- Reduced-Fat Margarine - 60g
- Fine Sugar - 125g
- Whole Egg, Fresh - 1 medium size
- Unsweetened Cocoa Powder - 10g
- Pure Vanilla Extract - 1 leveled teaspoon
- Low-Fat Plain Yogurt - 100g
- All-Purpose Flour - 150g, pre-sifted
- Baking Soda - ½ leveled teaspoon
- Distilled White Vinegar - ½ tablespoon
- Nonfat Milk - 2 tablespoons
- Reduced-Fat Cream Cheese - 150g
- Fat-Free Greek Yogurt - 75g
- Powdered Sugar - 1 tablespoon

Preparation Steps

- Heat your oven to 180°C (160°C if using a fan-assisted oven), which is equivalent to Gas Mark 4. Prepare a 12-cup muffin pan with liners.

- Cream together the reduced-fat margarine and fine sugar in a bowl using an electric mixer until the mixture is light and airy. Incorporate the whole egg and continue to mix until thoroughly blended. Sift the cocoa powder into the bowl, add the red gel food coloring (15g) and vanilla extract, and mix until uniform.

- Blend in half of the low-fat plain yogurt, then fold in half of the all-purpose flour, mixing vigorously. Repeat with the remaining yogurt and flour, beating for an additional 2 minutes until the batter is light and fluffy. Gently mix in the baking soda and distilled white vinegar on a low speed, then stir in just enough nonfat milk to achieve a batter that falls smoothly from a spoon.

- Evenly distribute the batter among the prepared muffin cups and bake for 20 minutes, or until the cupcakes have

- Pure Vanilla Extract - 1 leveled teaspoon

- risen and are springy to the touch. Allow them to cool slightly in the pan before transferring them to a cooling rack to cool completely.

- For the frosting, combine the reduced-fat cream cheese, fat-free Greek yogurt, powdered sugar, and vanilla extract in a small bowl. Once the cupcakes have cooled, garnish them with the frosting using a swirling motion.

Apricot, blueberry & nut crumble

6 Points

- Preparation Time : 10 min
- Cook Time : 25 min
- Total time : 35 min
- Servings : 6

Ingredients

- Low-Calorie Cooking Spray – 4 sprays
- Canned Apricots in Juice, Drained – 2 small cans (410g in total)
- Blueberries – 125g, previously frozen, thawed and drained
- Hazelnuts – 35g, finely ground
- Gluten-Free Self-Raising Flour (White) – 45g
- Ground Cinnamon – ½ teaspoon, level
- Light Brown Sugar – 2 tablespoons
- Reduced-Fat Margarine – 40g
- Almond Flakes – 25g

Preparation Steps

- Preheat your oven to 200°C (fan-assisted 180°C), gas mark 6. Use the low-calorie spray to lightly coat a baking dish with a 750ml capacity.

- Place the drained apricots and blueberries into the dish, spreading them out evenly.

- In a separate bowl, mix together the finely ground hazelnuts, gluten-free self-raising flour, cinnamon, and brown sugar. Work the reduced-fat margarine into the dry ingredients with your fingertips until the mixture takes on the texture of coarse breadcrumbs. Then, fold in the flaked almonds.

- Sprinkle the crumble mixture over the layered fruit in the dish.

- Bake in the preheated oven for 20-25 minutes, or until the topping turns golden brown and has a crunchy texture.

Edyth Breese

Cheat's trifle

6 Points

Preparation Time : 10 min
Cook Time : 5 min
Total time : 15 min
Servings : 4

Ingredients

- Fresh or Thawed Blackberries - 600 grams
- Non-nutritive Sweetener - 4 teaspoons
- Sugar-Free Gelatin Powder - 20 grams
- Crushed Rich Tea Biscuits - 4 pieces
- Light Whipped Cream (aerosol) - 60 grams
- Pre-made Vanilla Custard - 140 grams
- Multicolored Nonpareils - 1 portion, for garnish

Preparation Steps

- In a small saucepan, combine the blackberries with the non-nutritive sweetener and 4 tablespoons of water. Heat the mixture until it begins to simmer. Allow it to cook for 5 minutes, then gently mash the berries. Set aside to cool.

- Prepare the gelatin by dissolving the powder in 280 milliliters of boiling water. Then, incorporate an additional 280 milliliters of cold water. Allow the mixture to cool.

- Evenly distribute the gelatin into four serving glasses and place them in the refrigerator. When the gelatin is nearly set, sprinkle the crushed biscuit crumbs over it, followed by the cooled blackberry mixture. Return the glasses to the refrigerator to set completely.

- Once set, layer the vanilla custard on top of the blackberry layer, and finish with a dollop of light whipped cream.

- Garnish with multicolored nonpareils before serving.

The Weight Watchers Cookbook 2024

Plum Amaretto pudding

5 Points

- Preparation Time : 45 min
- Cook Time : 25 min
- Total time : 1 hr 10 min
- Servings : 6

Ingredients

- Fresh Plums – 450 grams, quartered and stones removed
- Cream Liqueur – 4 tablespoons of Amaretto, Marsala, or sweet sherry
- All-Purpose Flour – 110 grams
- Fine Salt – a small pinch
- Raw Egg – 1 medium-sized
- Skimmed Milk – 300 milliliters
- Pure Vanilla Extract – 1 teaspoon, leveled
- Fine Granulated Sugar – 1 tablespoon
- Low-Calorie Oil Spray – 5 pumps
- Powdered Sugar – 2 teaspoons, leveled

Preparation Steps

- Combine the plums with your choice of cream liqueur in a container. Seal and let them marinate for a minimum of 30 minutes, giving them a gentle mix now and then.

- Create the batter by whisking the all-purpose flour, a pinch of salt, the egg, skimmed milk, vanilla extract, and fine granulated sugar in a bowl. Let it rest, covered, while the plums are marinating.

- Warm the oven to a temperature of 200°C (392°F) for standard ovens or 180°C (356°F) for fan-assisted ovens, which corresponds to Gas Mark 6. Coat a 1.5-liter shallow baking dish with the low-calorie oil spray.

- After marinating, separate the plums from the liquid, making sure to keep the liquid. Place the plums into the greased dish, and then evenly distribute the prepared batter over them. Position in the middle of the oven and bake for 20-25 minutes until the pudding is firm and has a golden hue.

- Present the dessert with a drizzle of the saved marinating liquid and a dusting of powdered sugar. For a twist, consider substituting plums with fresh, pitted cherries.

The Weight Watchers Cookbook 2024

Toffee apple pie

7 Points

Preparation Time : 20 min **Total time : 1 hr**
Cook Time : 40 min **Servings : 4**

Ingredients

- Apple - 8 medium-sized, peeled, cored, and sliced

- Ground Cinnamon - ½ teaspoon, level

- Toffee Sauce (Sainsbury's brand preferred) - 3 tablespoons

- Reduced-Fat Spread - 40 grams

- Filo Dough - 3 sheets, large (approximately 25cm x 45cm each)

- Greek Yogurt (0% fat) - 4 tablespoons, for serving

Preparation Steps

- Begin by combining the sliced apples with the ground cinnamon in a saucepan, along with 75ml of water. Allow the mixture to simmer on medium heat for about 15 minutes, or until the apples have softened and the water has completely evaporated. Once cooked, place the apple mixture into a small, round baking dish and evenly pour the toffee sauce over it. Ahead of baking, preheat your oven to 190°C (fan-assisted 170°C), equivalent to gas mark 5.

- In a separate pan, gently melt the reduced-fat spread over a low flame. Take one sheet of the filo dough and lay it flat on a clean work surface. Lightly brush it with the melted spread, then crumple it gently and set it atop the apple mixture in the dish. Follow this process with the remaining filo sheets, ensuring the entire surface of the apple mixture is covered. Place the dish in the preheated oven and bake for 20 to 25 minutes, or until the filo topping turns crisp and achieves a golden hue. Serve the freshly baked pie warm, complemented by a dollop of the fat-free Greek yogurt.

Edyth Breese

Steamed lemon pudding

7 Points

Preparation Time : 15 min

Total time : 1 hr 45 min

Cook Time : 1hr 30 min

Servings : 8

Ingredients

- Cooking Spray with Controlled Calories - 4 spritzes

- Smooth Lemon Spread - 3 tablespoons, level

- Fresh Lemon - Zest of 1 lemon, peeled

- Reduced-Fat Margarine - 80 grams

- Fine White Sugar - 30 grams

- Whole Raw Eggs - 2 medium-sized, raw

- Self-Rising White Flour - 120 grams

- Baking Powder - 1 teaspoon, level

- Plain Low-Fat Yogurt - 75 grams

- Raw Egg Yolk - 1 medium-sized

- Fine White Sugar - 10 grams

- Custard Mix - 2 teaspoons, level

Preparation Steps

- Coat a 1-liter pudding mold with a low-calorie cooking spray, line the base with parchment paper, and add the smooth lemon spread and half of the lemon zest.

- Combine the reduced-fat margarine, fine white sugar, eggs, self-rising flour, baking powder, low-fat yogurt, and the remaining lemon zest in a bowl. Whisk until just mixed, then layer this batter over the lemon spread. Cover the mold with parchment paper and aluminum foil, securing it with string.

- Place the mold in a large saucepan on a trivet, pour boiling water to half the height of the mold, cover with a lid, and simmer for 1 hour and 30 minutes, replenishing water as needed.

- For the custard, whisk together the egg yolk, fine white sugar, and custard mix in a bowl until smooth. Heat the milk in a saucepan until steaming, then combine a small amount with the egg mixture. Return the mixture to the saucepan and cook on low heat for 15 minutes, stirring until it thickens to coat a spoon.

- Skim Milk - 170 milliliters

- After cooking, remove the pudding's coverings. The sponge should rebound when lightly touched. With oven mitts, place a plate over the mold and invert to unmold the pudding. Top with any remaining lemon spread and serve with the custard.

Apple & rhubarb crumble

9 Points

Preparation Time : 20 min
Total time : 1 hr 10 min
Cook Time : 50 min
Servings : 6

Ingredients

- Apples - 3 of medium size, peeled, cored, and cut into slices

- Rhubarb - 400 grams, cleaned and chopped into 2 cm sections

- Superfine Sugar - 2 tablespoons

- Orange - Grated zest from one orange

- Orange Juice - 45 milliliters, freshly squeezed

- All-Purpose Flour - 75 grams

- Margarine: 50 grams, diced into tiny pieces

- Soft Brown Sugar - 25 grams

- Rolled Oats - 75 grams

- Ready-to-Serve Low-Fat Custard - 1 large can

Preparation Steps

- Warm your oven to a temperature of 180°C (fan-assisted 160°C, gas mark 4). Combine the sliced apples, rhubarb, superfine sugar, and grated orange zest in a sizeable oven-safe dish. Integrate the fresh orange juice, then seal the dish with aluminum foil and bake for 25 minutes, or until the mixture is tender.

- During the baking period, take a mixing bowl and blend the all-purpose flour with the margarine until you achieve a crumbly texture akin to coarse breadcrumbs. Fold in the soft brown sugar and rolled oats, then evenly distribute this crumble mixture over the softened fruit.

- Continue to bake for an additional 25 minutes, or until the crumble turns a rich golden hue. Follow the heating instructions on the custard package and serve it alongside the hot fruit crumble.

- Carefully fold in the wholemeal self-rising flour, followed by the grated beetroot, ensuring it's well incorporated.

- Transfer the batter into the prepared baking tin, leveling the top for an even surface. Bake for 55 minutes to 1 hour. The brownies are ready when a skewer inserted into the center comes out with only a few crumbs attached.

- Take the tin out of the oven and set it on a cooling rack. Wait for the brownies to cool completely before removing them from the tin. Dust the top with unsweetened cocoa powder and slice into 20 even squares for serving.

Cranachan

5 Points

- Preparation Time : 10 min
- Total time : 15 min
- Cook Time : 5 min
- Servings : 4

Ingredients

- Rolled Jumbo Oats - 50 grams
- Level Tablespoon of Demerara Sugar - 1
- Fresh Raspberries - 250 grams
- Level Tablespoons of Honey - Approximately 2 and 2/3
- Tablespoons of Whisky or Bourbon - 3
- Greek Yogurt with 0% Fat - 350 grams

Preparation Steps

- In a medium-sized frying pan, gently heat the rolled jumbo oats and demerara sugar over a low to medium flame until toasted. Once done, remove from heat and put aside.

- Take 50 grams of raspberries and strain them through a mesh sieve into a small bowl, ensuring to discard the leftover seeds.

- In a different bowl, blend together six teaspoons of honey with the whisky/bourbon and the Greek yogurt. Keeping one tablespoon of the toasted oat mixture aside, incorporate the rest along with the strained raspberry puree into the yogurt blend.

- Assemble the dessert by creating layers in four individual serving glasses, starting with the whole raspberries and then adding the yogurt mixture on top.

- Finish each glass with a sprinkling of the reserved toasted oats and a half teaspoon of the remaining honey drizzled over the top.

The Weight Watchers Cookbook 2024

Vegetarian Options

Edyth Breese

- Shakshuka
- Sweet corn and Carrot Fritters
- Veggie Frittata Slice
- Caprese Panini rolls
- Veggie delight salad
- Veg and chilli tofu rolls
- Veggie hash with poached eggs
- Vegetarian lasagne
- Sweet and sour cauliflower with rice

Shakshuka

0 Points

- Preparation Time: 15 min
- Cook Time: 35 min
- Total time: 50 min
- Servings: 4

Ingredients

- Chopped Red Bell Pepper - 1 medium-sized
- Chopped Yellow Bell Pepper - 1 medium-sized
- Chopped Eggplant - 1 medium-sized
- Tomatoes, Diced in Can - 1 can (400 grams)
- Herb and Garlic Pizza Sauce - 1 tablespoon
- Cumin Powder: 2 teaspoons
- Sweet Paprika Powder - ½ teaspoon
- Crushed Dried Chili - 1 teaspoon
- Eggs - 4 medium-sized
- Fresh Cilantro Leaves - ½ cup
- Plain Fat-Free Yogurt (Unsweetened) - ⅓ cup (approximately 80 grams)

Preparation Steps

- Begin by coating a non-stick skillet lightly with cooking spray and warm it over a medium-high flame. Introduce the bell peppers and eggplant to the pan, along with 2 tablespoons of water. Stir the mixture and cook for about 10 minutes, or until the vegetables have softened.

- Next, incorporate the canned tomatoes, herb and garlic pizza sauce, ground cumin, sweet paprika, and dried chili flakes. Pour in an additional ½ cup (125 milliliters) of water and elevate the heat to bring the mixture to a rolling boil. Then, lower the heat to allow the mixture to simmer. Continue cooking for 15 to 20 minutes, or until the vegetables are thoroughly tender and the sauce has thickened.

- Create four depressions in the thick sauce using the back of a spoon. Gently crack an egg into each of these wells. Cover the skillet and let it simmer for another 5 to 6 minutes, or until the eggs have reached your desired level of doneness.

Edyth Breese

- Cooking Spray - 1 three-second spray
- To finish, garnish the dish with a scattering of fresh cilantro leaves. Serve the prepared dish accompanied by a side of unsweetened fat-free yogurt.

The Weight Watchers Cookbook 2024

Sweetcorn and carrot fritters

2 Points

Preparation Time : 20 min	Total time : 45 min
Cook Time : 25 min	Servings : 4

Ingredients

- Corn kernels from a can, washed and drained - one 420g can

- Large carrots, roughly shredded - two carrots; see tip for guidance

- Garlic clove, finely minced - one clove

- Ground cumin - one teaspoon

- Smoked paprika - two teaspoons

- White self-raising flour - half a cup or 75g

- Eggs, medium-sized - five eggs

- Natural yoghurt with no added fat - 100g, unsweetened

- Lemon juice - a quarter cup or 60ml

- Chickpeas from a can, washed and drained - two 400g cans

- Cherry tomatoes - 400g

- Small red onion, finely sliced

Preparation Steps

- Preheat the oven to 160°C and prepare a baking sheet with parchment paper

- In a sizable mixing bowl, combine the corn, grated carrots, minced garlic, and spices. Season with salt and pepper, then fold in the flour.

- Beat one egg lightly and incorporate it into the vegetable mixture thoroughly. Form the mixture into eight equal-sized patties and place them on a plate to rest.

- Use oil spray to lightly coat a large non-stick skillet and warm it over medium-high heat. Cook the patties in two batches, allowing each side about 3 minutes to turn lightly golden. Move the cooked patties to the baking sheet and keep them warm in the oven. Continue with the remaining patties.

- Clean the skillet and apply another light coating of oil spray. Cook the remaining eggs for 3-4 minutes, ensuring the egg whites set and the yolks remain soft.

Edyth Breese

- Fresh flat-leaf parsley, chopped - two tablespoons, plus additional for garnish

- Oil spray - two instances of a 3-second spray

- In a small bowl, mix the yoghurt with lemon juice and add salt and pepper to taste. In another bowl, toss together the chickpeas, cherry tomatoes, and red onion. Drizzle with the yoghurt mixture and sprinkle with parsley, tossing everything to blend.

- Present the fritters alongside the soft-cooked eggs and the refreshing chickpea salad, garnished with extra parsley.

The Weight Watchers Cookbook 2024

Veggie frittata slice

1 Points

Preparation Time : 20 min	Total time : 50 min
Cook Time : 30 min	Servings : 4

Ingredients

- Fresh baby spinach, approximately 6 cups (120g)
- Medium-sized eggs, a total of 7
- One medium carrot, shredded
- A medium zucchini, shredded
- One medium red bell pepper, finely diced
- Half of a medium red onion, sliced thinly
- Garlic cloves, 3 in number, minced
- All-purpose flour, about 15 grams

Preparation Steps

- Begin by preheating your oven to a temperature of 180°C (356°F). Prepare a baking dish measuring 20 by 30 centimeters by lightly coating it with oil and lining both the base and sides with parchment paper.

- Take a sizable bowl that is safe for microwave use, and place the spinach inside. Cover the bowl and microwave on high power for approximately 1 to 1.5 minutes, or until the spinach has wilted.

- Allow the spinach to cool for a brief period, then thoroughly drain it. After draining, exert pressure to eliminate any remaining moisture and give the spinach a coarse chop.

- In a separate large bowl, whisk the eggs until they are just combined. To the eggs, add the prepared spinach, shredded carrot, shredded zucchini, diced red bell pepper, thinly sliced onion, minced garlic, and flour. Season the mixture with a pinch of salt and freshly ground black pepper to taste, and stir everything together until it is uniformly mixed.

- Proceed to pour the vegetable and egg blend into the baking dish that has been prepared, and smooth out the top to ensure an even layer. Place the dish in the oven and bake for 30 minutes, or until the mixture has completely set.

- Once baked, let the dish stand for 5 minutes in the baking dish before slicing it into four equal portions. This dish can be served either warm or chilled, as per your preference.

The Weight Watchers Cookbook 2024

Caprese panini rolls

7 Points

- Preparation Time : 15 min
- Cook Time : 15 min
- Total time : 30 min
- Servings : 4

Ingredients

- Plant-based Mayo - 1 tbsp
- Artisan White Rolls - Four 60g rolls, sliced in half
- Ripe Tomatoes - Four large, cut into slices
- Fresh Basil Leaves - ¼ cup
- Cooking Spray - One 3-second spritz
- Dense Tofu - 250g
- Almond Beverage, No Sugar Added - 1 cup (250ml)
- Cornstarch - 2½ tbsp
- Savory Yeast Flakes - 10g
- Citrus Extract - 1 tsp

Preparation Steps

- Begin by creating the faux mozzarella. Combine the tofu, unsweetened almond beverage, cornstarch, savory yeast flakes, and citrus extract in a blender until the mixture achieves a creamy consistency.

- Move the blend to a saucepan and heat it over a medium flame. Whisk continuously for approximately 8 to 10 minutes, or until the mixture thickens. Distribute the thickened blend into two small molds and leave to cool. Then, refrigerate for 90 minutes or until it solidifies.

- Once set, unmold the faux mozzarella and slice it into 5mm discs. Keep these aside for later use.

- Apply a thin layer of plant-based mayo on the cut sides of the white rolls. Layer the bottom halves with tomato slices, fresh basil, and the prepared faux mozzarella.

- Season with a pinch of salt and pepper to taste. Place the top halves of the rolls on and give a light mist of cooking spray.

- Heat a grill or griddle to a medium-high temperature. Grill the assembled rolls in batches if necessary, for 2 to 3 minutes on each side.

- Apply pressure with a spatula to ensure even grilling until the faux mozzarella begins to soften and the rolls turn a golden brown color. Serve these hot off the grill.

The Weight Watchers Cookbook 2024

Veggie delight salad

5 Points

Preparation Time : 15 min	Total time : 30 min
Cook Time : 15 min	Servings : 4

Ingredients

- Prepared Pearl Barley - ⅓ cup (65 grams)

- Grated Zucchini - 1 small zucchini, coarsely grated

- Carrot Ribbons - 1 small carrot, sliced into ribbons

- Fresh Baby Spinach - 20 grams

- Sliced Red Bell Pepper - ¼ of a medium-sized pepper, thinly sliced

- Low-fat Cottage Cheese - ½ cup (125 grams)

- Chopped Avocado - ¼ of a small, ripe avocado, diced

- Alfalfa Sprouts - ¼ cup (10 grams)

- Extra Virgin Olive Oil - 1 teaspoon

- White Wine Vinegar - 1 tablespoon

Preparation Steps

- Assemble the ingredients by layering the cooked pearl barley, grated zucchini, carrot ribbons, baby spinach, sliced red bell pepper, low-fat cottage cheese, chopped avocado, and alfalfa sprouts in a container with a 3-cup (750ml) capacity, such as a glass jar or a plastic container.

- Create the dressing by combining extra virgin olive oil, white wine vinegar, and whole grain mustard in a small mixing bowl.

- Whisk the mixture until it is well-blended. Season the dressing with salt and pepper to taste.

- When ready to serve, pour the dressing over the layered salad.

- Whole Grain Mustard - 1 teaspoon

The Weight Watchers Cookbook 2024

Veg and chilli tofu rolls

4 Points

- Preparation Time : 20 min
- Total time : 30 min
- Cook Time : 10 min
- Servings : 4

Ingredients

- Olive oil - 2 teaspoons
- Firm tofu - 250 grams
- Sambal oelek - 2 teaspoons
- Low-sodium soy sauce - 2 tablespoons (combine 1 tablespoon Tamari with another tablespoon for dipping)
- Wombok (Chinese cabbage) - 200 grams, finely sliced
- Rice paper sheets - 120 grams (12 pieces, each 22 cm in diameter)
- Snow peas - 150 grams, finely sliced
- Carrot - 1 large, julienned
- Fresh mint leaves - ¼ cup
- Avocado - 1 large, cut into slices

Preparation Steps

- Warm the olive oil in a wok on high heat. Sauté the tofu for 2 to 3 minutes until it achieves a golden hue. Incorporate the sambal oelek and Tamari, stirring to evenly coat the tofu. Allow the mixture to cool for 5 minutes in a separate dish after mixing in the shredded wombok.

- Soften each rice paper wrapper by submerging it in hot water for 10 to 20 seconds. Lay it out on a clean dishcloth to remove any surplus moisture. In the center of each softened rice paper, place a portion of the tofu mix, followed by a small amount of the shredded snow peas, carrot sticks, mint leaves, and avocado slices.

- Neatly fold over the edges of the rice paper and roll it tightly to secure the contents. Continue this process with the remaining wrappers and filling ingredients until you have created 12 rolls.

- Present the rolls with additional Tamari on the side for dipping.

Edyth Breese

Veggie hash with poached eggs

3 Points

Preparation Time : 40 min
Total time : 55 min
Cook Time : 15 min
Servings : 4

Ingredients

- Large new potatoes, 600 grams, halved

- Zucchini, 2 medium-sized, sliced lengthwise and then crosswise

- Yellow bell pepper, 1 medium, sliced into slender wedges

- Chopped fresh thyme, 1 teaspoon, plus additional for garnish

- Red onion, 1 medium, sliced into thin wedges

- Cherry tomatoes, 200 grams, halved

- Eggs, 4 medium

- Chopped fresh basil, 2 tablespoons, with additional leaves for garnish

- Finely chopped fresh flat-leaf parsley, 2 tablespoons

- Cooking spray, for two brief spritzes

Preparation Steps

- Boil the halved potatoes in a pot of water for 10 minutes, or until they are slightly tender, then drain and set aside to cool.

- In a large mixing bowl, toss the zucchini, bell pepper, and thyme together. Mist lightly with cooking spray to coat.

- Spray a sizable non-stick skillet with cooking spray and warm over a medium-low flame. Sauté the onion for 6-8 minutes until it becomes translucent. Introduce the boiled potatoes and the zucchini mixture to the pan, seasoning with salt and pepper. Add a small amount of water, cover, and let cook for 15 minutes or until the potatoes are fully cooked.

- Take off the cover, turn up the heat, and stir-fry for about 4 minutes until the vegetables begin to caramelize. Transfer the vegetables back into the bowl. In the same pan, cook the cherry tomatoes for 1 minute until they are slightly softened, then mix them with the other vegetables and set aside.

- Simultaneously, heat a large, deep skillet of water until boiling, then lower the heat. Gently slide each egg into the water one at a time. Poach the eggs for 1-2 minutes until the whites are firm but the yolks remain runny. Use a slotted spoon to remove the eggs, draining them on a paper towel-lined plate.

- Fold the basil and parsley into the vegetable mix. Plate the vegetables and top each serving with a poached egg. Garnish with extra thyme and basil leaves before serving.

Vegetarian lasagne

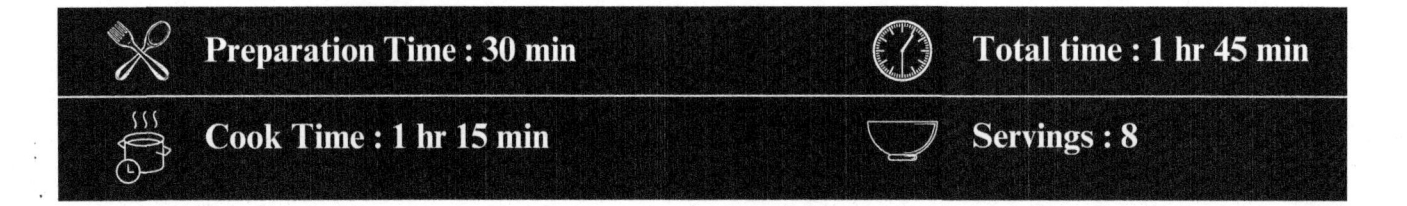

3 Points

- Preparation Time : 30 min
- Cook Time : 1 hr 15 min
- Total time : 1 hr 45 min
- Servings : 8

Ingredients

- Chopped Brown Onion (1 medium-sized)
- Diced Eggplant (1 medium-sized, cut into 1cm cubes)
- Chopped Red Bell Pepper (1 medium-sized, cut into 1cm pieces)
- Sliced Zucchini (1 medium-sized, cut into 1cm pieces)
- Cubed Butternut Squash (300g, peeled and cut into 1cm pieces)
- Minced Garlic (2 cloves)
- - Chopped Tomatoes in Juice (1 can of 400g)
- Tomato Puree (700g)
- Fresh Spinach (4 cups or 80g)
- Ground Nutmeg (¼ tsp)
- Smooth Low-Fat Cottage Cheese (2 cups or 500g)

Preparation Steps

- Warm your oven to 180°C. Using a large non-stick saucepan, apply a brief spray of cooking oil and set over a medium-high flame. Introduce the onion, eggplant, bell pepper, zucchini, and squash, cooking for 5 minutes with occasional stirring. Infuse with half the garlic, a pinch of salt and pepper, and continue to stir for 2 more minutes. Fold in the canned tomatoes, tomato puree, and 375ml of water. Elevate to a boil, then lower the heat, cover, and let it simmer for 30 minutes, stirring now and then.

- In the meantime, place a large non-stick frying pan over a medium flame. Combine the remaining garlic, spinach, nutmeg, and a tablespoon of water. Stirring continuously, cook until the spinach has wilted. In a food processor, whip the cottage cheese for 30 seconds until it reaches a smooth texture. Introduce the spinach mixture and pulse 3-4 times until just mixed.

- Pour 1 cup of the simmered vegetable medley into the base of a 32cm x 20cm (12-cup capacity) baking dish. Create a foundation with lasagna noodles, then

- Wholemeal Lasagna Noodles (250g, uncooked)
- Shredded Light Mozzarella Cheese (2 tbsp)
- Fresh Basil Leaves (¼ cup, for garnish)
- Cooking Spray (for a 3-second spray)

- overlay with ¼ of the remaining vegetable blend. Continue to layer with the remaining noodles and vegetables, ending with a final layer of noodles. Crown the assembly with the blended cottage cheese and scatter mozzarella on top.
- Bake for 40-45 minutes or until the lasagna sheets are soft when probed with a knife tip. Let the lasagna rest for 10 minutes prior to serving. Garnish with fresh basil leaves.

Edyth Breese

Sweet and sour cauliflower with rice

8 Points

- Preparation Time : 10 min
- Total time : 35 min
- Cook Time : 25 min
- Servings : 4

Ingredients

- 1 large cauliflower, separated into florets
- 1 small red onion, sliced into wedges
- 1 medium red bell pepper, sliced into 3cm pieces
- 1 medium green bell pepper, sliced into 3cm pieces
- 2 cloves of garlic, thick slices
- 1½ teaspoons of canola oil
- 1½ tablespoons of light soy sauce
- 1½ tablespoons of cornstarch
- ¼ cup (60ml) of ketchup
- 430g of canned pineapple chunks in natural juice, drained (reserve juice)
- 150ml of no added sugar pineapple juice
- 2 tablespoons of rice wine vinegar

Preparation Steps

- Heat your oven to 200°C and line a baking sheet with parchment paper. Arrange the cauliflower, red onion, red and green bell peppers, and garlic on the sheet. Drizzle with canola oil and toss to ensure an even coating. Roast for 20 minutes or until the vegetables have softened.

- In a small container, blend the soy sauce with cornstarch. Over medium heat, transfer this blend to a large non-stick skillet or wok. Gradually whisk in the ketchup, the 150ml of reserved pineapple juice, rice wine vinegar, and 350ml of water.

- Heat the mixture until it reaches a boil, then lower the heat and let it simmer for 4-5 minutes, or until the sauce thickens. Introduce the roasted vegetables and half of the pineapple chunks to the skillet. Stir for about a minute, ensuring the vegetables are well-coated with the sauce.

- Serve the sweet and sour cauliflower over the heated basmati rice, divided into bowls. Garnish with the sliced green onions.

- 2 cups (340g) of cooked basmati rice, warmed

- 2 green onions, thinly sliced

Edyth Breese

The Weight Watchers Cookbook 2024

Diabetes Friendly Recipes

Edyth Breese

- Banana berry parfait
- Creamy oat porridge with apple and blueberries
- Buckwheat pancakes with honeyed ricotta
- Honey and ginger chicken stir-fry
- Coconut pancakes
- Dark chocolate avocado cake
- Greek-inspired chicken burgers
- Strawberry and cottage cheese muffins
- Easy chicken curry

The Weight Watchers Cookbook 2024

Banana berry parfait

2 Points

Preparation Time : 10 min **Total time : 10 min**
Cook Time : 0 min **Servings : 4**

Ingredients

- Bananas, 2 large (cut into slices)

- Raspberries, fresh, 20 pieces

- Strawberries, fresh, 12 pieces (cut in halves or quarters)

- Natural muesli with nuts, seeds, and dried fruit, ½ cup (approximately 55 grams)

- Yogurt, 99% fat-free and unsweetened, 1 cup (about 240 grams)

- Brown sugar, 2 teaspoons

Preparation Steps

- Begin by evenly distributing the sliced bananas, fresh raspberries, and strawberry pieces into four serving glasses or bowls, each with a 1-cup (250ml) capacity. Follow by adding a layer of natural muesli over the fruit.

- Proceed to spoon the unsweetened, 99% fat-free yogurt on top of the muesli layer. Finish by sprinkling the brown sugar over the yogurt.

- Allow the assembled parfaits to rest for approximately 5 minutes, giving the brown sugar time to dissolve into the yogurt. Once ready, serve and enjoy

Creamy oat porridge with apple and blueberries

3 Points

Preparation Time : 5 min
Cook Time : 10 min
Total time : 15 min
Servings : 1

Ingredients

- Quick-Cooking Oats, Uncooked – ⅓ cup (30g)
- Low-Fat Cottage Cheese – ⅓ cup (80g)
- Apple, Finely Diced – ½ of a medium apple
- Fresh Blueberries – ¼ cup (40g)
- Ground Cinnamon – ½ tsp

Preparation Steps

- Begin by placing the quick-cooking oats into a small saucepan along with 1 cup (250ml) of boiling water. Continuously stir the mixture over a medium flame for approximately 4 to 5 minutes, or until it starts to boil and the texture becomes thicker. Afterward, remove the saucepan from the heat, cover it, and let it rest for 5 minutes, or until the oats achieve a thick and creamy consistency. Then, pour the oats into a breakfast bowl.

- In a separate bowl, blend half of the low-fat cottage cheese with 1 tablespoon of water until you achieve a smooth consistency. Fold this mixture into the prepared oats until fully integrated. Incorporate the majority of the diced apple into the oat mixture.

- For the final touch, garnish the oatmeal with the fresh blueberries, the remaining diced apple, and dollops of the leftover cottage cheese. To complete the dish, lightly dust the top with ground cinnamon before serving.

Buckwheat pancakes with honeyed ricotta

6 Points

- Preparation Time : 10 min
- Total time : 25 min
- Cook Time : 15 min
- Servings : 4

Ingredients

- Buckwheat Flour - 75 grams (approximately 1/2 cup)
- Whole Wheat Self-Rising Flour - 50 grams (about 1/3 cup)
- Baking Powder - 1/2 teaspoon
- Cinnamon, Ground - 1/2 teaspoon
- Granulated Sugar - 1 tablespoon
- Egg - 1 medium-sized
- Skimmed Milk - 250 milliliters (1 cup)
- Low-Fat Ricotta Cheese - 1/3 cup
- Honey - 2 teaspoons
- Fresh Mixed Berries - 200 grams
- Cooking Spray Oil - One 3-second spray

Preparation Steps

- Begin by combining both the buckwheat and whole wheat self-rising flours with the baking powder and ground cinnamon through a sieve into a medium-sized mixing bowl. Incorporate the granulated sugar by stirring it in. In a separate container, whisk together the milk and egg until they are well mixed. Create a well in the center of the dry ingredients and pour in the liquid mixture. Whisk everything together until the batter is smooth and free of lumps, then let it rest for 10 minutes.

- In the meantime, prepare the ricotta by blending it with the honey in a small bowl until they are thoroughly mixed.

- Prepare a large non-stick skillet by lightly coating it with cooking spray oil and warm it over a medium flame. Pour 60 milliliters (1/4 cup) of the batter into the pan for each pancake.

- Allow the pancake to cook for 1 to 2 minutes, or until bubbles form on the surface, then flip it to cook for an additional 1 to 2 minutes, or until the pancake turns a golden brown color.

- Move the cooked pancake to a plate and cover it to keep it warm. Continue this process with the remaining batter, cooking multiple pancakes simultaneously if possible, until you have a total of 8 pancakes.

- To serve, top the warm pancakes with the honey-ricotta mixture and garnish with the fresh berries.

The Weight Watchers Cookbook 2024

Honey and ginger chicken stir-fry

7 Points

- Preparation Time : 20 min
- Total time : 35 min
- Cook Time : 15 min
- Servings : 4

Ingredients

- Grated Fresh Ginger - 2 tablespoons (from a 5 cm piece)

- Pure Honey - 2 tablespoons

- Soy Sauce - 1 tablespoon

- Sriracha - 2 teaspoons

- Crushed Garlic Cloves - 2 cloves

- Lime Juice - 1 tablespoon

- Chicken Breast (without skin) - 600 grams, cut into 3 cm chunks

- Medium Carrot - 1 piece, shaved into thin ribbons with a vegetable peeler

- Broccoli Florets - 350 grams, cut small

- Chopped Fresh Coriander - 2 tablespoons

- Brown Rice (cooked) - 2 cups (340 grams)

Preparation Steps

- In a substantial bowl, blend the grated ginger, honey, soy sauce, sriracha, crushed garlic, and lime juice. Introduce the chicken pieces, coating them thoroughly with the mixture. Allow to marinate briefly.

- Apply a light coating of cooking spray to a sizable non-stick skillet or wok. Set over a high flame to heat. Sauté the carrot ribbons and broccoli florets for approximately 4 to 5 minutes or until they reach a tender state. Transfer the vegetables to a plate and keep them aside.

- Respray the skillet with a bit more cooking spray and warm it once again over a high setting.

- Cook the marinated chicken and any excess marinade, stirring frequently, for around 5 to 6 minutes or until the chicken is nicely browned and fully cooked.

- Reintroduce the vegetables to the skillet, warming them through. Take the skillet off the heat and fold in the chopped coriander.

Edyth Breese

- Lime - ½, sliced into wedges for garnish

- Cooking Spray - 2 applications of 3 seconds each

- Plate the stir-fry alongside the cooked brown rice and garnish with lime wedges to serve.

The Weight Watchers Cookbook 2024

Coconut pancakes

3 Points

Preparation Time : 10 min | **Total time : 30 min**

Cook Time : 20 min | **Servings : 12**

Ingredients

- Coconut Flour - 90 grams (approximately ⅔ cup)
- Baking Powder - 1 and ¼ teaspoons
- Large Eggs - 4
- Skim Milk - 250 milliliters (1 cup)
- Brown Sugar - 55 grams (¼ cup)
- Vanilla Extract (Alcohol-Free) - ¼ teaspoon
- Coconut Oil - 1 tablespoon, melted

Preparation Steps

- Combine the coconut flour, baking powder, and a pinch of salt (approximately ¼ teaspoon) in a small mixing bowl.

- In a separate, larger bowl, thoroughly mix the eggs, milk, brown sugar, vanilla, and 3 teaspoons of melted coconut oil. Gradually incorporate the dry ingredients into the wet mixture. Allow the batter to rest for 5 minutes to thicken modestly.

- Warm a sizable non-stick skillet over a medium flame. Use a bit of the leftover coconut oil to lightly grease the pan. Ladle the batter into the pan, using ¼ cup portions to form the pancakes. Allow them to cook for about 3 minutes, or until the bottom side is golden and the surface starts to firm up. Carefully flip the pancakes and continue cooking for an additional 2 to 3 minutes, until they achieve a nice golden brown color. If the pancakes are browning too rapidly, lower the heat. Apply a light coat of oil to the pan as needed, and proceed to cook until you have a total of 12 pancakes.

Edyth Breese

Dark chocolate avocado cake

6 Points

- Preparation Time : 20 min
- Cook Time : 30 min
- Total time : 50 min
- Servings : 16

Ingredients

- Chopped Dark Chocolate - 90g
- All-Purpose Flour - 1 cup (150g)
- Unsweetened Cocoa Powder - ½ cup (45g)
- Baking Powder - 2 tsp
- Baking Soda - ¾ tsp
- Fine Granulated Sugar - ¾ cup (165g)
- Unsweetened, Non-fat Plain Yogurt - 1 cup (240g)
- Half of a Medium Avocado, diced
- One Medium Egg
- Alcohol-free Vanilla Extract - 1 tsp
- Extra Cocoa Powder for dusting - 1 tsp
- Additional Non-fat Plain Yogurt for serving - ⅓ cup (80g)

Preparation Steps

- Preheat your oven to 180°C (350°F). Prepare a 20cm round baking tin by lightly coating it with oil and lining the bottom and sides with parchment paper. Gently melt the dark chocolate in a heatproof bowl set over a pot of simmering water, stirring occasionally, for about 2-3 minutes until smooth. Remove from heat to cool.

- In a large mixing bowl, combine the all-purpose flour, unsweetened cocoa powder, baking powder, baking soda, and a pinch of salt. Mix in the fine granulated sugar.

- In a food processor, blend the non-fat plain yogurt and diced avocado until the mixture achieves a smooth consistency. Incorporate the egg and vanilla extract with a few quick pulses, ensuring not to overmix.

- Fold the avocado-yogurt blend and the slightly cooled melted chocolate into the dry ingredients, stirring until the batter is thoroughly mixed. Transfer the batter into the prepared cake tin, leveling the top with a spoon.

- Bake in the preheated oven for 30 minutes, or until a toothpick inserted into the center of the cake comes out clean. Allow the cake to cool in the tin for 10 minutes before moving it to a wire rack to cool completely.

- Prior to serving, lightly dust the cake with additional cocoa powder and serve each slice with a spoonful of non-fat plain yogurt.

Edyth Breese

Greek-inspired chicken burgers

6 Points

- Preparation Time : 20 min
- Cook Time : 6 min
- Total time : 26 min
- Servings : 4

Ingredients

- Boneless Chicken Breast (4 pieces, 125g each)
- Extra Virgin Olive Oil (2 teaspoons)
- Red Wine Vinegar (1 teaspoon)
- Chopped Fresh Dill (1 teaspoon)
- Ground Dried Oregano (½ teaspoon)
- Garlic Powder or Flakes (¼ teaspoon)
- Low-Fat Feta Cheese (80 grams)
- Skimmed Milk (3 teaspoons)
- Finely Diced Red Onion (from ¼ of a medium onion)
- Baby Cos Lettuce Leaves (from 4 heads)
- Medium White Bread Rolls (4 pieces, 50g each), halved and toasted

Preparation Steps

- Begin by placing the chicken breasts between two sheets of plastic wrap. Use a mallet to pound them gently until they reach a uniform thickness of 1cm. Arrange them in a wide, shallow container.

- In a separate small bowl, combine the olive oil, red wine vinegar, chopped dill, oregano, and garlic powder. Season with salt and pepper to taste, then whisk the mixture together. Drizzle this marinade over the chicken, making sure to coat both sides thoroughly. Allow the chicken to marinate for 10 minutes.

- Preheat a grill pan over medium-high heat and lightly coat with cooking spray oil. Once hot, grill the chicken for approximately 2-3 minutes per side, or until it achieves a slight char and is fully cooked.

- While the chicken is cooking, take a small bowl and combine the feta cheese, skimmed milk, and chopped red onion. Use a fork to mash these ingredients together until you achieve a spreadable consistency.

- Medium Tomato, Sliced (1 piece)
- Cooking Spray Oil (for a 3-second spray)

- To assemble, arrange a layer of baby cos lettuce leaves on the bottom halves of the toasted bread rolls. Add a piece of grilled chicken on top of each. Spread the feta cheese mixture over the chicken, then add a slice of tomato. Finish by placing the top halves of the rolls on top to complete the sandwiches.

Strawberry and cottage cheese muffins

1 Points

- Preparation Time : 15 min
- Cook Time : 30 min
- Total time : 45 min
- Servings : 12

Ingredients

- Fresh Medjool Dates - 12 units, pitted and coarsely chopped
- Baking Powder - 2 teaspoons
- Low-Fat Cottage Cheese - 1 cup (250 grams)
- Rolled Oats - 2 cups (180 grams)
- Eggs - 3 medium-sized
- Pure Vanilla Extract, non-alcoholic - 2 teaspoons
- Ripe Strawberries - 250 grams, thinly sliced

Preparation Steps

- Begin by heating your oven to 180°C (350°F). Prepare a muffin pan with 12 slots, each with an 80 ml capacity, by lining them with muffin papers.

- In a sizable bowl safe for microwave use, mix the chopped dates with 2 tablespoons of hot water. Cover the bowl and microwave on the highest setting for 90 seconds. Add the baking powder to the softened dates, which will cause the mixture to bubble up.

- In a food processor, blend the cottage cheese until it achieves a smooth consistency. Incorporate the oats, eggs, vanilla extract, and the date mixture by processing them together until just mixed, being careful not to overdo it to maintain a light texture. Fold in 200 grams of the sliced strawberries with a few quick pulses.

- Distribute the batter evenly among the muffin cups. Sprinkle the tops with the remaining strawberry slices, gently pressing them into the batter. Bake for 30 minutes, or until the muffins turn a golden color and a skewer inserted into the middle comes out clean.

- Allow the muffins to cool in the pan for 5 minutes before moving them to a cooling rack. These muffins can be enjoyed warm or at room temperature.

Edyth Breese

Easy chicken curry

6 Points

- Preparation Time : 20 min
- Total time : 50 min
- Cook Time : 30 min
- Servings : 4

Ingredients

- Olive Oil (1 tablespoon)
- Boneless Chicken Thighs (450 grams, with fat removed and chopped; purchase 500 grams)
- Medium Brown Onion (1, finely chopped)
- Garlic Cloves (2, minced)
- Fresh Ginger (2 teaspoons, finely grated)
- Ground Coriander (1 and 1/2 teaspoons)
- Ground Turmeric (1/2 teaspoon)
- Ground Cayenne Pepper (1/4 teaspoon)
- Diced Tomatoes in Juice (400 grams can)
- Light Coconut Milk (125 milliliters)
- Pumpkin (300 grams, peeled and diced into 2-centimeter cubes)

Preparation Steps

- In a sizable saucepan set over a medium flame, warm the olive oil. Sauté the chicken in two separate portions, stirring occasionally, for 4 minutes per portion or until each piece is nicely browned. Place the chicken aside once browned.

- In the same saucepan, sauté the onion, stirring it occasionally, for about 5 minutes or until it turns soft and takes on a golden hue. Mix in the minced garlic, grated ginger, ground coriander, and other spices, and continue to stir for another 30 seconds.

- Reintroduce the chicken to the saucepan. Incorporate the diced tomatoes, 180 milliliters of water, and the coconut milk.

- Add the pumpkin and cauliflower pieces to the mix. Cover the saucepan and allow the contents to reach a gentle simmer.

- Continue to cook with the lid partially on for 15 minutes, or until the vegetables are fork-tender and the chicken is thoroughly cooked.

- Cauliflower (300 grams, separated into florets)
- Frozen Green Peas (120 grams)
- Chopped Fresh Coriander (2 tablespoons)
- Lime (1, cut into wedges for serving)

- Add the green peas and let them cook for an additional 2 minutes or until they are soft. Garnish the dish with chopped fresh coriander. Serve the meal accompanied by lime wedges.

The Weight Watchers Cookbook 2024

Smoothie Recipes

The Weight Watchers Cookbook 2024

- Chocolate-pineapple protein smoothie
- Chocolate-strawberry protein smoothie
- Vanilla-strawberry protein smoothie
- Chocolate-banana protein smoothie
- Apple & greens smoothies
- Cherry-almond smoothies
- Chocolate Almond & Cherry Smoothie
- Creamy corn smoothie

The Weight Watchers Cookbook 2024

Chocolate-pineapple protein smoothie

3 Points

- Preparation Time : 3 min
- Cook Time : 0 min
- Total time : 3 min
- Servings : 1

Ingredients

- Whey Protein Powder with Chocolate Flavor (1 scoop)
- Cold Water (12 fluid ounces)
- Pineapple Chunks (½ cup, can be either fresh or frozen)

Preparation Steps

- In a blending appliance, add the chocolate-flavored whey protein powder, cold water, and pineapple chunks. If utilizing fresh pineapple, consider including a handful of ice cubes to achieve a chilled consistency.
- Blend the mixture until it reaches a smooth texture.
- This recipe yields one serving.

Chocolate-strawberry protein smoothie

3 Points

- Preparation Time : 3 min
- Total time : 3 min
- Cook Time : 0 min
- Servings : 1

Ingredients

- Whey Protein Powder (Chocolate Flavor) - 1 serving
- Cold Water - 12 fluid ounces
- Fresh Strawberries - ½ cup
- Ice Cubes - 4 pieces

Preparation Steps

- In a blending apparatus, amalgamate the whey protein powder, chilled water, strawberries, and ice cubes.

- Blend the mixture until it achieves a rich and velvety consistency. This recipe yields a single portion.

The Weight Watchers Cookbook 2024

Vanilla-strawberry protein smoothie

3 Points

- Preparation Time : 2 min
- Total time : 2 min
- Cook Time : 0 min
- Servings : 1

Ingredients

- Whey Protein Powder with Vanilla Flavor (1 scoop)
- Chilled Water (12 fluid ounces)
- Fresh Strawberries (1 cup), tops removed
- Ice Cubes (4 pieces), optional

Preparation Steps

- In a blending apparatus, amalgamate the whey protein powder, chilled water, fresh strawberries, and ice cubes if desired.
- Blend the mixture until it achieves a rich and smooth consistency. This recipe yields a single portion.

Edyth Breese

Chocolate-banana protein smoothie

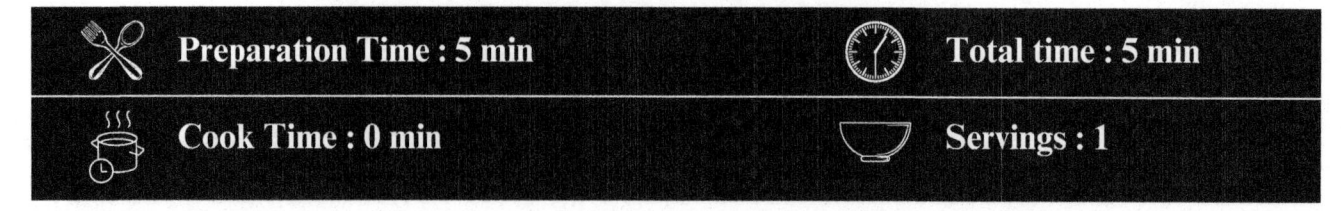

6 Points

Preparation Time : 5 min	Total time : 5 min
Cook Time : 0 min	Servings : 1

Ingredients

- Whey Protein Powder (Chocolate Flavor) - 1 scoop
- Cold Water - 6 fluid ounces
- Skimmed Milk (Fat-free) - 6 fluid ounces
- Ripe Banana - ½ of a large banana
- Ice Cubes - 4

Preparation Steps

- In a blending device, amalgamate the whey protein powder, cold water, fat-free skim milk, half a large ripe banana, and ice cubes.

- Blend the mixture until it achieves a thick and creamy consistency. This recipe is tailored for a single serving.

Apple & greens smoothies

5 Points

- Preparation Time : 5 min
- Cook Time : 0 min
- Total time : 5 min
- Servings : 2

Ingredients

- Spinach (baby variety), 2 cups
- Greek yogurt (non-fat, plain), 1 cup
- Almond milk (unsweetened, plain), 3/4 cup
- Honeycrisp apple (or similar variety), 1 small, core removed and roughly chopped
- Banana, 1 small, previously frozen and cut into slices

Preparation Steps

- Utilize a high-powered blender to blend all the listed components until the mixture achieves a smooth consistency, which should take approximately 30 seconds to 1 minute.
- Suggested Portion: Roughly 1 and 2/3 cups per serving.

Cherry-almond smoothies

4 Points

- Preparation Time : 5 min
- Total time : 5 min
- Cook Time : 0 min
- Servings : 2

Ingredients

- Sour red cherries, frozen and without added sugar (1½ cups)
- Cauliflower rice, uncooked and frozen (1 cup)
- Almond milk, plain and unsweetened (1 cup)
- Tofu, firm consistency (3 ounces)
- Almond butter, in powdered form without added sugar (¼ cup)
- Pure almond extract (⅛ teaspoon)

Preparation Steps

- Combine the sour red cherries, cauliflower rice, almond milk, firm tofu, powdered almond butter, and almond extract in a blending apparatus.
- Blend on a high setting until the mixture achieves a smooth consistency, which should take approximately 30 seconds to 1 minute.

Chocolate Almond & Cherry Smoothie

6 Points

- Preparation Time : 10 min
- Total time : 10 min
- Cook Time : 0 min
- Servings : 2

Ingredients

- Dark sweet cherries, unsweetened and frozen - 1.5 cups
- Cauliflower, riced and uncooked - 1 cup, preferably frozen
- Almond milk, plain and unsweetened - 1 cup
- Almond butter, unsweetened and in powder form: 0.25 cups
- Extract of almond - 0.25 teaspoons
- Tofu, extra firm - 3 ounces
- Cocoa powder, without added sugar - 3 tablespoons

Preparation Steps

- Commence by placing all the components, excluding the cocoa powder, into a blending machine.

- Proceed to liquefy the mixture at a high setting until a uniform consistency is achieved, which should take between 30 seconds and a minute.

- Proceed to apportion half of the resulting smoothie into two 16-ounce glasses. Introduce the cocoa powder into the blender containing the residual smoothie mixture and blend once more to ensure the cocoa is fully integrated, which should require an additional 30 seconds.

- With care, pour the chocolate-infused smoothie atop the almond-cherry blend in the glasses, creating a dual-layered effect.

Creamy corn smoothie

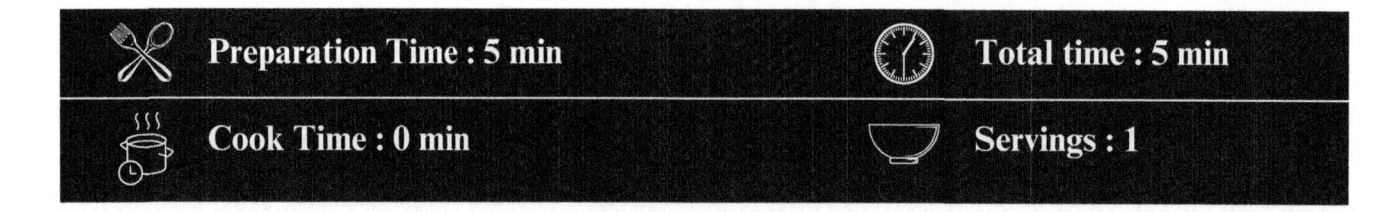

4 Points

- Preparation Time : 5 min
- Total time : 5 min
- Cook Time : 0 min
- Servings : 1

Ingredients

- Yellow corn, canned - ½ cup(s)
- Greek yoghurt, fat free, plain - ½ cup(s)
- Packed brown sugar - 1 Tbsp
- Vanilla extract - ½ tsp
- Ice cube - ¼ cup(s)

Preparation Steps

- Combine the yogurt, sugar, vanilla and ice in a blender.
- Blend until the mixture achieves a smooth consistency.
- Makes 1 serving

Conclusion

In closing the "Weight Watchers Cookbook 2024," reflect on the essential elements that have enhanced your quest for a healthier lifestyle. Throughout this book, you've embarked on a culinary adventure, uncovering dishes that delight the senses while adhering to Weight Watchers' principles.

From wholesome breakfast, lunchtime delights, dinner feasts to veggies options, diabetes friendly recipes and smoothie recipes, every recipe has been designed with your health as a priority. The SmartPoints framework has steered your decisions, promoting conscious eating and igniting a passion for cooking that marries taste with nutritional value.

As you turn the final page, let these principles resonate in your approach to food. Embrace the harmony of taste and health, find pleasure in feeding your body well, and enjoy the fulfillment that comes from conscious culinary choices. Your path to improved health is paved with these intentional, small steps.

Looking forward, consider this book not just as a collection of recipes but as a guide on your continued wellness journey. Keep up the progress you've made, explore new flavors, and value the happiness derived from intentional nourishment.

Here's to a future rich in wellness, contentment, and the ongoing delight of eating mindfully. I am grateful for your participation in this delectable quest.

Edyth Breese

Your Feedback Matters!

Dear Esteemed Readers,

I trust that you have found pleasure and inspiration within the pages of the "Weight Watchers Cookbook 2024," and that it has offered you exciting and healthful culinary options. The perspectives and opinions you provide are of great significance to me, as they enable me to refine and tailor my work to better serve your interests.

I kindly request that you spare a moment to convey your impressions, whether they pertain to the recipes you most enjoyed, areas for enhancement, or the impact the cookbook has had on your approach to cooking. Your contributions are not only beneficial to me but also enrich our shared culinary narrative.

I am grateful for your participation in this shared path to health and well-being. Your input and time are highly valued.

Wishing you joy in your culinary endeavors!

Edyth Breese.

Printed in Great Britain
by Amazon

The Weight Watchers Cookbook 2024 is your guide to a transformative culinary experience that reshapes your relationship with food and well-being. Explore a scrumptious collection of recipes that adhere to Weight Watchers' trusted methods, promoting a harmonious and conscious way of eating. From satisfying morning dishes to tempting sweet treats, each recipe is a tribute to taste and vitality.

This cookbook goes beyond mere calorie tracking; it's your roadmap to making wise, lasting dietary decisions that feed both your physique and spirit. Adopt the versatility of the SmartPoints system, relish the benefits of ZeroPoint foods, and commence a journey to wellness that transcends the numbers on the scale.

Allow the Weight Watchers Cookbook 2024 to spark your culinary creativity, crafting mouthwatering dishes that turn each mouthful into a stride towards a more balanced and enriching way of life. Get ready to celebrate the path to wellness with the pure pleasure of cooking.